THE BATTLE FOR THE BRITISH GRAND PRIX

THE BATTLE FOR THE
BRITISH
GRAND
PRIX

THE INSIDE STORY OF THE FIGHT TO
SAVE BRITAIN'S BIGGEST MOTOR RACE

ALAN HENRY

Haynes Publishing

First published in July 2010

A catalogue record for this book is available from the British Library

ISBN 978 1 84425 974 8

Library of Congress catalog card no 2010921835

Published by Haynes Publishing,
Sparkford, Yeovil, Somerset BA22 7JJ, UK
Tel: 01963 442030 Fax: 01963 440001
Int.tel: +44 1963 442030 Int.fax: +44 1963 440001
E-mail: sales@haynes.co.uk
Website: www.haynes.co.uk

Haynes North America Inc.,
861 Lawrence Drive, Newbury Park, California 91320, USA

Designed and typeset by James Robertson

Printed and bound in the USA

CONTENTS

ACKNOWLEDGEMENTS

I would like to offer my appreciation to the British Racing Drivers' Club and John Blunsden of Motor Racing Publications for permission to quote from *Silverstone: Fifty Glorious Years*, which was published exclusively for club members in 1998. I would also like to thank Sir Jackie Stewart and Headline Publishing for permission to quote from Sir Jackie's official autobiography, *Winning Is Not Enough*. Thanks also to Maurice Hamilton for helping with excellent source material from his volume *British Grand Prix*.

At the BRDC thanks are also due to chairman Robert Brooks and secretary Stuart Pringle. Thanks also for chats over recent years on this subject to Sir Jackie Stewart, Damon Hill, Martin Brundle, Martin Colvill, Tommy Sopwith, John Foden and David Brodie, not to mention my fellow board directors from 2004 to 2006, Stuart Rolt, Tony Jardine, Jackie Oliver, Michael Ostroumoff, Mike Knight, John Cardwell, Mark Blundell and Ray Bellm, all of whom were on the receiving end of the membership's critical review for much of that time. All I can say is that it was certainly more difficult than it may have looked from the touchlines.

For anybody who wants to read more on the subject of Bernie Ecclestone, I would unhesitatingly recommend *Bernie Ecclestone: King of Sport* by Terry Lovell, which has been most useful for checking the events leading up to the negotiation of Silverstone's five-year contract to run the British Grand Prix from 2005, the period when I was one of the club's directors, and the subsequent fiasco surrounding the ill-starred attempt to move Britain's round of the F1 world championship to Donington Park. Really, the whole sorry saga was a story you couldn't have made up.

Alan Henry
Tillingham, Essex
2010

PROLOGUE

It is one of those spine-tingling experiences that never fails to excite. Take a stroll away from the Silverstone paddock on the outside of the circuit and you eventually arrive at the braking point for Copse corner. Well, it used to be the braking point. Nowadays a more apposite appellation would be 'turning-in point'. It is a place to marvel at the raw aerodynamic downforce, sheer power, and speed of the contemporary grand prix car.

It matters not which generation you are referring to. Whether it be Alberto Ascari stylishly steering his Ferrari 500 to victory in 1953, Jim Clark languidly laying the oh-so-elegant Lotus 49 into the long turn 14 years later, or the explosive fire power of Nigel Mansell's stupendous Williams FW14B trashing the opposition on the way to victory in 1992.

Generations of F1 fans have their own personal stories about what Silverstone and the British Grand Prix mean to them. There are those whose high spot of the weekend was standing on a muddy track-side bank, eating their ham sandwiches from a greaseproof paper package prepared by their mothers. Almost inevitably, it was raining on these dyed-in-the-wool, passionate enthusiasts who were the seed corn on which the sport's heritage and appeal were founded over the decades. It was much like being on convoy duty around North Cape.

At the other end of the spectrum are the polished high rollers, millionaires, celebrities, and sponsors' five-star business guests who peopled – and continue to people – the exclusive Paddock Club, where they could dally over their stuffed prawns and Chardonnay as Michael Schumacher and his rivals strutted their high-octane stuff within yards of their cut glass and freshly laundered napkins. A goodly mix, as you might say.

The British Grand Prix has long been an essential cornerstone of the UK's annual sporting calendar. Right up there with Ascot, the Henley Regatta, and Wimbledon, it is a touchstone for the country's technical diversity and competitive spirit. Yet its story is not simply an account of high-octane endeavour and deeds of derring-do. The race has been subject to a turbulent history and tortured process of evolution that, in so many ways, tracks the very history of F1 itself.

This is the story of how Britain's most important motor race grew in stature over more than five decades, from a relatively small-time sport, growing from 'blokes messing around with racing cars' into a highly sophisticated money-making machine that accurately reflected the tone of a brazenly commercial era as spearheaded by Bernie Ecclestone.

Ecclestone, who started his business life running a motorcycle and car sales business in south London, had himself once been a racing driver in the 500cc category during the early 1950s.

This might add a piquant sense of irony to the fact that, for a seemingly large slice of the history of the British Grand Prix, Ecclestone has apparently been at loggerheads with Silverstone and, more specifically, its owner, the British Racing Drivers' Club. The tensions and complexities of this relationship will be examined in detail between these covers, but at this early stage in the narrative let's just say that, in Ecclestone's F1 world, it is a matter of 'my way or the highway'. Pretty much, anyway.

Ecclestone is seldom out of the news. His status as one of the UK's richest and most successful businessmen ensures this remains virtually taken as read.

Far-sighted and shrewd, as well as a businessman of ferocious determination, Ecclestone eventually constructed a business empire that would generate upwards of $1 billion in annual revenues from race sanctioning fees, track-side advertising, and corporate hospitality.

Ecclestone successfully parlayed this crock of gold into an immense personal fortune for himself and his family when he sold his stake in the F1 business to CVC Capital Partners in 2005 for a mind-boggling $478 million. As a result of this deal, the future prosperity of the F1 business was mortgaged by becoming linked to a bond that, in turn, was secured against the board's future commercial revenues.

The mathematics of this intricate agreement directly affected F1 grand prix organisers in general and the British Grand Prix in particular. Ecclestone, always one to drive a hard bargain, missed no opportunities during the final decade of the 20th century to ramp up the individual race sanctioning fees. Dissenters were briskly reminded that if they didn't want to sign on the dotted line for their race, there were plenty who would. A succession of government-backed race organisers in Malaysia, Bahrain, China, Abu Dhabi, and South Korea was effectively able to write blank cheques for the privilege of joining the grand prix club. As we shall see, for the promoters of the British Grand Prix at Silverstone, commercial reality was very different indeed.

Silverstone was not born with a silver spoon in its corporate mouth. It always had to make its motor racing pay. That meant balancing the books, year in and year out. Yet increasingly this was easier said than done, with the financial margins continually being eroded as the race promoters were required to pay more and more money for the privilege of holding their race while, at the same time, their own scope for making any cash to top up their depleted reserves was continually trimmed and restricted.

This story is necessarily, but not exclusively, principally about how Silverstone, the circuit that held the first post-war British Grand Prix in 1948, battled through the rigours of a changing F1 world to secure Britain's round of the world championship on a long-term basis from 2010. Aintree and Brands Hatch are major supporting characters in this drama, with Donington Park having a walk-on role towards the end of this story of corporate and sporting ducking and diving.

CHAPTER ONE

WHERE IT ALL BEGAN

How a Second World War RAF aerodrome sowed the seeds as the self-styled 'home of British motor racing' by staging the first post-war British Grand Prix in 1948. The story of the track's early years, in which it staged the British Grand Prix uninterrupted through to 1954.

Silverstone was literally put on the map during the depths of the Second World War. According to the British Racing Drivers' Club (BRDC) archives, a heavy bomber aerodrome equipped with five large hangars was built for the Royal Air Force (RAF) by civil engineers Mowlem at a reported cost of £1,112,565. It was conceived with a main 6,000ft (roughly one-mile) runway positioned north–south, with intersecting runways of 3,900 and 4,200ft (roughly half and three-quarters of a mile). Crucially for its subsequent metamorphosis into a makeshift race track in the immediate post-war years, the design also incorporated a perimeter track three miles in length.

RAF Silverstone's main function was as a training establishment during its two-year operational wartime life, which began in April 1943. Wellington, Halifax, and Lancaster bombers taxied along the runways and perimeter roads that would one day reverberate to the crackling roar of F1 cars on full song. In total around 8,600 air crew were trained at Silverstone and its satellite aerodrome, Turweston.

Silverstone ceased to be operational at the end of 1946 and was declared a 'surplus inactive station' in October of the following year.

The immediate post-war years were gruelling, hard, and uncompromising for the people of the UK. Rationing would last well into the 1950s and the worst winter weather for a century virtually caused the country to grind to a halt under a nationwide blanket of snow during the early months of 1947. Yet beneath this unwelcome veneer of austerity, a small group of enthusiasts wanted to revive motor racing in some form or another and they were determined that their enthusiastic spirit should not be snuffed out. Many of the potential participants had fought on active service and were adamant that they would continue to be involved in a pastime that would keep their adrenalin pumping during their peacetime leisure activities.

To say that the first race – make that 'event' – to take place at Silverstone was informal and non-sanctioned would be to stray into the realms of understatement. Of course, there was no prospect of reviving Brooklands, the epic banked track near Weybridge, which had long since been surrendered to the aviation industry, and Donington Park remained under the control of the War Ministry as one of the biggest military vehicle dumping grounds in the country. Ironically, the future of Donington Park and Silverstone would become briefly and controversially intertwined in 2009 in one of the most complex episodes surrounding the future destiny of the British Grand Prix.

One weekend in September 1947 a group of Frazer Nash enthusiasts who had been attending a hill climb at Shelsley Walsh decided to have their own impromptu race meeting at

Silverstone the following day. They were set to compete on a makeshift track approximately two miles long when sheep straying on to the rutted asphalt perimeter road forced them to abandon their plans.

The following month a group of 500 Club members tried their luck, arriving at the entrance to the old aerodrome with Wing Commander Frank Aiken, who had served at the base during the war, and Colin Strang, Clive Lones, Eric Brandon, John Cooper – whose family's F1 cars would race to two world championships in the hands of Jack Brabham little more than a decade later – and Lord David Strathcarron. They were turned away, only for Lord Hesketh – Alexander Hesketh's father – to invite them to make practice runs along the private roads within his Easton Neston estate at nearby Towcester. Twenty-seven years later, James Hunt would win the BRDC International Trophy race at Silverstone driving Alexander's Cosworth-engined Hesketh 308.

Meanwhile, the competitions committee of the Royal Automobile Club (RAC), the chairman of which was the BRDC's president Earl Howe, was continuing its search for something that could become a fully fledged motor racing facility in the UK. Eventually the search was narrowed down to Snitterfield, near Stratford-upon-Avon, and Silverstone. The tenacious RAC grandees were put in touch with Sir Peter Masefield, then working for the Ministry of Aviation, where he was much involved in the disposal of the many RAF aerodromes scattered around the country. He duly granted the RAC a one-year lease on Silverstone.

The RAC convened a press conference at its London headquarters on 30 June 1948, at which it introduced Colonel

Stanley Barnes as its new competitions manager. But there was more. Wilfred Andrews, the RAC chairman, not only revealed the club's plans to take a lease on Silverstone, but also confirmed plans to hold the track's first British Grand Prix on 2 October, just three months later. It was a hugely ambitious step to take, the first of many audacious decisions in the long march to consolidating Silverstone as the self-styled home of British motor racing.

For those who moaned and complained over the decades that followed about the sodden car parks and long queues that became part of the Silverstone experience for loyal race fans, it could be said without fear of contradiction that the 1948 grand prix certainly set the tone of things to come. Little thought was given to spectator facilities. Indeed, with the RAC leasing the track only on an annual basis, there was no serious incentive to develop permanent facilities. And that state of affairs would continue substantially unchanged for many years.

Hazel Morgan, the wife of RAC committee member John Morgan, memorably recounted just how primitive the toilet facilities were in those early Silverstone days. After finally reaching the front of a very long queue for the ladies' toilets, she was sitting in the cubicle when she suddenly became aware of a draught and a sudden "relaxation of the gloom around [her] legs".

"There you are, love," said a cheerful male Cockney voice. "A nice clean bucket for yer", and the cubicle darkened again as the flap behind the bucket closed.

Not only were the facilities primitive, but it was noted by many competitors that the race's senior officials, some of whom had been in positions of authority in the services during the war, seemed now to be lacking in the sympathetic touch when it came to the tactful handling of voluntary staff who had been recruited to assist during the weekend.

In fact, Bob Ansell, who competed in that first Silverstone grand prix at the wheel of a Maserati, recalled many years later that there was very nearly a drivers' strike over the race weekend. Each competitor had invested the large sum of £20 as an entry fee, but they were subsequently irked to discover that the works Maserati team was being paid very respectable starting money – even though the team did not turn up until practice was over.

Earl Howe successfully defused the threat of a drivers' strike by assuring the competitors that, if they managed to complete one lap of the race, their entry fees would be returned.

All in all, it was a low-key start to Silverstone's grand prix heritage. The 'San Remo' 4CLT/48 Maserati driven by the popular Swiss Emmanuel de Graffenried emerged the winner after the similar cars of 'Bira' and Luigi Villoresi retired, both having earlier led the race.

However, as journalist and author John Blunsden shrewdly noted, 'The euphoria at finally being able to go motor racing again could not disguise the dismay of drivers who were called upon to race towards each other from opposite ends of a runway before peeling off at an intersection lined with straw bales.'

Roy Salvadori, whose Maserati was one of just 10 finishers out of the 25-car field, recalled that "it really was appalling". He added, "Fortunately, they abandoned using the runways after that and confined the racing to the perimeter roads, which is when the real Silverstone came into being."

But not before there was one more important modification. A tight S-bend was added to the track layout at Club corner for the 1949 grand prix to slow the cars before they reached the fast left-hand Abbey Curve. This had been widely condemned by competitors because it brought cars down to a slow crawl, over-taxing their brakes and tyres and sending several drivers into the straw bales used to define the deviation.

In 1950 a conventional corner was re-established at Club, producing a configuration that would remain essentially unchanged for the next 25 years. The circuit would become loved by a wide cross-section of drivers, its high-speed flow more than making up for the relative flatness of the topography.

"I first raced there in 1955," remembered triple world champion Sir Jack Brabham with great affection, "and I loved it. It was so quick it was really exhilarating. But you had to be very precise with your line, especially through Club. You had to stay on the left on the approach so as to cut across to a late apex on the right, otherwise you'd run wide on the exit as the track fell away and your lap would be ruined."

In 1949 the future of Silverstone would be assured to a large degree as the result of a meeting that took place on 4 October at the Fleet Street headquarters of Beaverbrook Newspapers, the owners of the *Daily Express*.

Tom Blackburn, the general manager of Beaverbrook Newspapers, summoned the motoring correspondent Basil Cardew to his office and suggested in characteristically direct fashion that if a reputed 100,000 fans were prepared to queue for hours to watch an event on a disused aerodrome, then surely the *Express* should be supporting such a sport. "I want you to organise a motor race for the *Daily Express*," he told the hapless Cardew.

It's a sign of just how different things were in those days that the RAC proved to be unbelievably sniffy about the whole idea, which reeked far too much of commercial exploitation. "Press sponsorship of RAC events is undesirable", ran the snooty official line. Reportedly in despair, the well-connected Cardew sought out his old friend Desmond Scannell, the secretary of the BRDC, which operated out of a tiny office in Mayfair.

Scannell immediately agreed that the BRDC would stage a race meeting for the *Express*, but then highlighted a rather sobering thought. The club had only £13 10s in its bank account. A meeting was speedily arranged between Scannell and Tom Blackburn and thus was born the *Daily Express* International Trophy event, which would grow into one of the most prestigious non-championship races on the calendar.

The BRDC is very much regarded as custodian of motor racing's bloodline and heritage in Great Britain, its history rooted in a very different era. It was in the late 1920s that the eminent bacteriologist Dr Dudley Benjafield, one of the famed 'Bentley Boys' who competed with distinction at Le Mans, organised a series of dinner parties from which modest beginnings the club was born.

It was officially inaugurated in 1928 with an initial membership of just 25 and a clearly defined sense of purpose. This included a commitment to promote the interests of motor sport generally, to celebrate any specific performance in motor sport, to extend hospitality to racing drivers from overseas, and to further the interests of British drivers competing abroad.

More than 80 years on, those sentiments may seem quaintly phrased, but their core values are essentially unchanged. Today the BRDC casts its net wide when it comes to encouraging and conserving all that is best in British motor racing, whether this means encouraging young talent through the club's wide-ranging initiatives, or looking after the best interests for the future of Silverstone, the home of British motor racing, the freehold of which the club purchased from the Ministry of Defence in 1971.

The entry criteria to the club remain exacting. Full membership is offered only to those ladies and gentlemen who have achieved international motor racing success over a number of seasons. Associate membership is offered to those who, although not qualifying for full membership, have made an exceptional contribution to the sport. Honorary membership is for a special few, including F1 champions, who do not otherwise qualify.

Back in 1950, however, the BRDC had yet to develop into the commercial powerhouse it has become today. Its remit was rather more modest. For that season the Fédération International de l'Automobile (FIA) had devised the first official world championship contest, which would be run over seven 'classic' races with the British Grand Prix at Silverstone opening the series. Even more exciting for the bigwigs at the RAC, King George VI and Queen Elizabeth accepted an invitation to attend on the day, ensuring that the event would be an occasion to savour.

The royal party had its own grandstand on the start–finish straight, fitted out with gilded armchairs and decorated with bunting and roses. Later they moved to a specially constructed vantage point positioned to give them a closer view of the on-circuit action, before leaving the circuit and returning to London in the royal train from the station at Brackley, now long defunct. The race itself was dominated by the works Alfa Romeos, with Giuseppe Farina taking the win, as he would in the International Trophy race three months later.

The first BRDC International Trophy meeting had certainly been a success when it took place on 20 August 1949. As part of the deal the RAC, as Silverstone's leaseholder, took a healthy 33 per cent of the gate receipts; it was a good deal as things transpired, because this was to be hailed as Britain's most successful motor race, with more than 100,000 spectators cramming through the gates.

Appropriately enough, Farina received his second Silverstone trophy of the 1950 season from Lord Beaverbrook's son Max Aitken, an RAF Spitfire hero who had won a Distinguished Service Order and double Distinguished Flying Cross for his exploits during the war. Aitken was a motor racing fan who had raced a Bugatti under a nom de plume at Brooklands during the war in order to avoid the disapproval that he, perhaps correctly, anticipated from his father.

The 1951 British Grand Prix hosted the world championship debut of the immensely complicated, controversial, and generally unreliable British Racing Motors (BRM) P15s in the race at Silverstone. Reg Parnell finished fifth, two places ahead of Peter Walker in the other BRM, much to the delight of the UK crowd.

'No praise can be enough for their unforgivable performance,' wrote the legendary John Bolster in *Autosport* magazine. He rounded off what might be described as an over-approving assessment by writing, 'In conclusion, I would like to thank Reg Parnell for consenting to give me a broadcast interview when he was in great pain from his burns.'

As an interesting aside, the British Grand Prix 500cc supporting race was won in superb style by the young rising star Stirling Moss. Farther back in 10th place was one B.C.

Ecclestone. Half a century later anyone wanting a 'broadcast interview' with any F1 driver would be doing so through Mr Ecclestone's Formula One Administration empire.

Although Britain's economy seemed to be emerging slowly from the post-war depression during the early 1950s, the future of major sporting events such as the British Grand Prix still seemed far from securely guaranteed. The RAC's race organising sub-committee was getting seriously worried about the costs of the event, having originally allocated £10,000 in starting money and £1,500 for prizes, only to find that Ferrari alone wanted £1,800 to bring three cars.

The RAC's reaction was one of outrage, particularly as the 'nationally owned' Alfa Romeo squad was asking for only around half that figure. Nevertheless, the organisers decided that, despite the cost, the grand prix would not be complete without Ferrari and they planned to invite only two cars, not three, for Alberto Ascari and Luigi Villoresi. They did not originally extend the invitation to the burly Froilan González, who ended up winning the race to give the Prancing Horse its maiden world championship grand prix victory at the wheel of the 4.5-litre V12-engined naturally aspirated Ferrari Tipo 375.

Despite the fact that Silverstone had successfully hosted an epic event, the RAC was now minded seriously to re-think its position towards Silverstone and the British Grand Prix and it later emerged that, even before the 1951 fixture took place, it had decided not to renew the circuit lease for the following year.

As it was reported by *Autosport* magazine on 25 May 1951, 'The RAC has announced that it will not renew the lease on Silverstone airfield circuit after the present year. Whilst the club is most anxious for such facilities as have existed at Silverstone and elsewhere to continue, it has come to the conclusion that it is most inappropriate that it should continue to remain lessee of a motor racing circuit, and that in retaining the lease, it may deter other interested and suitable bodies, who would be acceptable to the authorities, making arrangements of a more permanent character there or elsewhere.'

It seems that Goodwood was later dismissed as an unsuitable venue for Britain's premier motor race, rather a hard judgement on a circuit that would come to be regarded as one of the most popular of UK tracks in the years that followed. But the BRDC would not let the grass grow under its feet and, with the financial backing of the *Daily Express*, the club was quick to explore the possibility of taking over the lease on Silverstone.

As part of the potential fund-raising exercise, members were asked if they would dig deep into their pockets and make interest-free loans in a bid to raise £5,000. By October 1951 the BRDC had an agreement in principal to take over and the RAC duly announced that it would delegate the organisation of the 1952 race to the club.

From the moment the BRDC began its negotiations to assume the lease of Silverstone, it quickly focused on how best to upgrade the circuit to make it easier to operate and safer to race on, and generally to offer a more enjoyable experience for the paying spectators.

Committee member Kenneth Evans, a surveyor by profession who had raced as an enthusiastic amateur before the war, was charged with overseeing the modifications, a major feature of which would be the relocation of the start line, race control, and pits from their original site near Abbey Curve to the straight between Woodcote and Copse, where they were to remain until the inauguration of a new complex between Club and Abbey before the 2011 British Grand Prix.

The proposed work also included resurfacing sections of the track, digging ditches, and constructing earth banks on the outsides of corners. As far as the circuit length was concerned, widening and easing the line at Copse and Becketts changed the lap length to 2.927 miles. This revised layout also offered the secondary benefit of opening up the prospect of using a shorter, 1.608-mile club circuit by utilising the runway between Becketts and Woodcote, which could use the same start line and pits area as the grand prix track.

As part of the administrative reorganisation, the RAC's track manager Jimmy Brown moved across to the BRDC's employ to carry out the same job and – amusingly, in the light of what a big-budget sport F1 would eventually become – the club also decided to employ a gateman "provided he is proficient in first aid".

However, despite pleas from high places, the British motor industry did not seem interested in using Silverstone as a test track to aid the development of road cars. In the BRDC's silver jubilee year, at the club's annual general meeting, its president-in-chief the Duke of Edinburgh made a plea to this effect, but it went largely unheeded. Admittedly Jaguar, Rover, tractor manufacturer Ferguson, and Notwen Oils made donations of various vehicles to be used at the track, but the car makers as a whole concentrated their efforts on developing the Motor Industry Research Association on another old wartime airfield close to Nuneaton.

In 1952 and 1953, the FIA decided that the shortage of fully fledged F1 cars left it with little choice but to announce that, for these two seasons, the world championship should be run for 2-litre F2 machines. Both seasons were utterly dominated by Alberto Ascari at the wheel of a four-cylinder Ferrari 500; he won consecutive British Grands Prix at Silverstone on his way to back-to-back title crowns.

At the end of the 1953 season the BRDC committee took the opportunity to seriously review its position as a race promoter. At this time the *Daily Express* took full financial responsibility for the major meetings while handing over to the club any surplus profit generated. Even so, there was no guarantee that the grand prix would continue to take place at Silverstone on an open-ended basis.

Concerns were heightened by the news that a motor racing circuit was being constructed at Aintree, on the site of the horse racing course that staged the Grand National. The Aintree management had formed an alliance with the British Automobile Racing Club (BARC) and was lobbying the RAC to run the race at the Liverpool circuit.

By September 1954, two months after González had won his second British Grand Prix at Silverstone for Ferrari, the BRDC formally learned that the RAC had indeed invited the BARC to run the 1955 British Grand Prix at Aintree. This was a disappointment, but BRDC secretary Desmond Scannell was more than generous about the move. "It is fair that another club and venue be selected," he stated without any trace of rancour.

However disappointing this state of affairs may have seemed in the short term, it at least gave Silverstone a little financial breathing space. The costs of staging the British Grand Prix were steadily increasing, with the major European F1 teams intensifying their appearance money demands year on year. By the same token, there were other potential income streams to be exploited. When in 1955 the BBC agreed a deal for sound and television rights for all Silverstone events, the fee payable to the BRDC was fixed at £1,000.

There were also some lighter moments at Silverstone. In 1954 the BRDC received a letter from the RAC asking for an undertaking that helicopters not be allowed to land at the British Grand Prix meeting because of an unspecified 'incident' the previous year. Nevertheless, Sir Max Aitken, the vice-chairman of Beaverbrook Newspapers, arrived at the 1954 Grand Prix in one of these then-rare flying machines. One fan wrote to *Autosport* magazine noting that 'when that infernal machine is hovering around, no-one can hear a word coming over the public address system'.

It was a tough time for Silverstone and international motor racing in general throughout 1955. The Le Mans disaster – in which more than 80 people died – cast a long shadow across the sport, although there was a ray of brightness for British interests with Stirling Moss scoring the first grand prix victory of his career at Aintree at the wheel of the Mercedes W196.

The Silverstone fraternity could at least console itself with the fact that Aintree failed to draw as large a crowd as had attended the previous year's British Grand Prix, although the news value of Stirling's win at the head of an amazing Mercedes one-two-three-four certainly put the Liverpool circuit firmly on the map.

For the sake of decency I will not dwell on the comments of the late Denis Jenkinson, celebrated *Motor Sport* continental correspondent and the co-driver on Stirling's amazing run to victory in that year's Mille Miglia: "When I think of Aintree, I think of the smell from the urinals," he told me a few years before his death in 1996.

Those who queued in the rain for a makeshift 'comfort break' at Silverstone during the 1950s and 1960s might have been forgiven if they harboured similarly uncharitable thoughts.

In 1956 the grand prix made its way back to Silverstone, although it was the BRDC International Trophy meeting that really hit the headlines.

Although Moss was Maserati team leader contracted to drive in all the world championship *grandes épreuves*, he was free to drive for Vanwall in any non-championship events not contested by the Italian manufacturer. He duly won the International Trophy but the British Grand Prix a few months later fell to the Lancia Ferrari of Juan Manuel Fangio.

That same year, John Eason-Gibson took over as secretary of the BRDC after the retirement of Desmond Scannell.

The lingering effects of the Suez crisis resulted in the postponement of the 1957 International Trophy meeting. Although the political and military tension in this Middle East hot spot had passed its worst by the end of 1956, it was not for another couple of months that the situation really returned to normal. An alternative date was arranged for the autumn.

On a wider motor sporting horizon, the first flickering signs of F1 drivers and race organisers marshalling themselves into negotiating groups to protect their own interests began to emerge during the 1957 season. For the men behind the wheel, the Professional International Drivers' Association was established to give the drivers a voice when it came to circuit safety and other related matters. This was the forerunner of the

Grand Prix Drivers' Association for which future BRDC president Jackie Stewart became such a stalwart campaigner on safety issues a decade or more later.

In addition, at the beginning of the season, race organisers got together to investigate whether it was realistically feasible to standardise starting money arrangements for the grands prix, obviously at a rate rather lower than the teams were pressing for.

In those tranquil pre-Bernie days the whole episode turned out to be something of a stand-off and there was even some doubt that the official world championship would be able to muster the requisite half-dozen qualifying rounds if the project pressed ahead to a conclusion.

Eventually the organisers' rather fanciful attempts at unity fell apart, although it is interesting to reflect on the relatively modest figures involved. The proposal called for world champions to be paid £180 per race and each so-called 'grade one' driver £100. As far as the teams were concerned, it was suggested that £700 should be paid for each Ferrari and Maserati, £540 for each Vanwall, and £350 for the others.

The 1957 season was also marked by the passing of Dr Dudley Benjafield, that huge enthusiast who had been one of the key founding fathers of the BRDC and shared the winning Bentley at Le Mans in 1927. He was 69. In many ways, on reflection, this book could appropriately have been called 'From Benjy to Bernie'.

The British Grand Prix continued its somewhat nomadic existence throughout the late 1950s and into the 1960s, but there were other secondary problems with which the BRDC found itself grappling by the time Peter Collins won the 1958 British GP at Silverstone driving a Ferrari Dino 246. Relations with the farmer whose business involved land on both the inside and outside of the circuit were tense and slightly uncomfortable, and it seemed likely that things would run more smoothly if the club had control of the whole site.

As a result, during the summer of 1958, negotiations were initiated with the Ministry of Agriculture with a view to acquiring the lease on the farm land. As John Blunsden wrote in *Silverstone: Fifty Golden Years*, 'Even if the intention was to use more of the site for racing and related activities, this meant that the club had to become a farmer.

'Peter Clarke, a BRDC committee member with broad business experience, proposed that the farm should be operated separately by a limited company owned by the club. In time the farm would become a profitable subsidiary which would help support the racing activities.

'Silverstone needed to have a stronger commercial structure because the *Daily Express*, which had effectively run the business since 1949, announced that it was withdrawing its overall sponsorship, though it would continue to support individual events and provide advertising and publicity.'

Yet at the end of the day, it would be Silverstone that proved itself to be commercially stronger and more unyieldingly committed to the future security of F1 racing in Britain and would endure through to the next century as the powerhouse of UK motor racing. Not that it did not have some lurid challenges to face as the decades unfolded.

CHAPTER TWO

AINTREE INTERLUDE AND ON TO BRANDS HATCH

The years of sharing the race, first with Silverstone alternating with Aintree – through to 1962 – and then Brands Hatch taking over as the alternating host from 1964 to 1986. The politics and the finances.

The switch to Aintree for 1955 brought the F1 fraternity into contact with the Topham family, which owned the Liverpool race course that had become so famous as the home of the Grand National. Back in 1949 Tophams Ltd, the family holding company, had paid a staggering £275,000 to purchase the 260-acre site from the Earl of Sefton.

The Tophams were hard-edged entrepreneurs who realised that the public wanted to be entertained and looked after, not just stuck out in the rain waiting for something to happen – which, with all due respect to Silverstone and Brands Hatch, was then an all-too-familiar scenario at too many motor racing venues.

The Topham family's marketing of the Grand National was one of the biggest sporting commercial success stories of the 1950s and emergent television coverage ensured that it was screened to viewers throughout the world. But Aintree's arrival in the ranks of F1 venues came about as the result of an almost chance meeting.

In 1953, the redoubtable Mrs Mirabel Topham, the powerful

matriarch and business brains of the family, paid a visit to Lord March's Goodwood estate, where horse and motor racing took place, albeit at very different facilities a few miles apart. As a result of this visit the Tophams formed the Aintree Automobile Racing Company with the intention of improving profitability at the race course. A three-mile circuit was laid, the construction being completed in three months for a cost of £100,000, and the first event took place at the track on 29 May 1954.

The highlight was the so-called Aintree 200, which would establish itself as one of the most important non-championship F1 events to be staged in the UK alongside the Silverstone International Trophy, the Oulton Park Gold Cup, and the Brands Hatch Race of Champions, although the last-named event would not be inaugurated until 1965, the year after international racing at Aintree ceased.

Stirling Moss well remembers that meeting, which, like so many events at the Liverpool circuit, started in heavy rain. He won the 500cc race in his Beart-Cooper Mk VIIA and went on to repeat that success by taking first place in the F1 event at the wheel of his Maserati 250F. "The cars ran in anti-clockwise direction, although this would be reversed for subsequent meetings."

When in 1955 Stirling won the Aintree British Grand Prix for Mercedes, it seemed as though both the event and the outcome had been a huge success for both the track owners and the BARC, which had organised the event. But an extraordinary churlish broadside against the event was mounted by *Motor Racing* magazine, which was affiliated to the rival British Racing and Sports Car Club (BRSCC).

As Maurice Hamilton noted in *British Grand Prix*, these critics went straight for the jugular. One wrote, 'This was the first time the British Grand Epreuve had been run at Aintree, and if some people have their way it will also be the last. There is some justification for the public and private criticism which has been levelled at this Aintree meeting, but it was the first major event to be held there and many of the faults can be rectified if the owners are willing to go to the trouble of satisfying the wishes of the paying public.

'In the main the criticisms were mainly connected with the amenities provided for the prices charged, particularly those "out in the country". The paddock arrangements at Aintree are bad, the dust-laden atmosphere caused by cars and people moving over the loose ash surface is not popular with anybody but most particularly with mechanics trying desperately to keep oil filters and carburettors clean. The paddock is also too far removed from the race track from which it is totally isolated.'

If you thought this was the end of the criticism, you would have been mistaken. Not only did *Motor Racing*'s correspondent think that the circuit was lacking in terms of overall facilities, but he also slated the local Liverpudlians as being rather charmless: 'The complaints levelled at Aintree as a circuit may have been influenced, and made more pronounced, by Liverpool's treatment of visitors. Throughout the Liverpool area it seemed that visitors were no longer welcome. Good food was not obtainable, good service did not exist, good manners by the hotel and restaurant staffs was something that we should apparently not expect.'

Aintree, of course, would deliver another memorable victory for Stirling two years later at the wheel of the Vanwall, sharing the winning machine with his compatriot Tony Brooks. It was truly a seminal moment in post-war motor racing history and the Liverpool circuit's owners were proud that such a long-awaited great day should unfold so spectacularly on their turf.

Stirling recalled the day in great detail within the pages of his book *All My Races*: 'Fortunately, I recovered [from a sinus infection picked up while water skiing] in time for the British Grand Prix at Aintree, where we were clearly going to have strong opposition from Maserati, with Fangio and Behra faster than the Vanwalls on the first day's practice. Even though I was still feeling the after-effects of the sinus problem, I managed to qualify on pole position, right at the end of the session.'

Stirling had also taken the precaution of trying Brooks's car in practice and it was tacitly agreed that Tony, who was still recovering from injuries sustained at Le Mans, would be prepared to relinquish his car to Moss should it become strategically necessary. And that was precisely how the race unfolded, with Stirling's original car developing a misfire and, after two pit stops, Stirling taking over Brooks's car and returning to the fray in ninth place.

Moss continued his account of the run to the chequered flag: 'Just as I passed Stuart Lewis-Evans's Vanwall for third place, the clutch disintegrated on Behra's leading Maserati and Hawthorn's second-placed Ferrari suffered a punctured tyre running over the debris...

'I took no chances in the closing stages. I even made a precautionary late stop to top up with fuel. The car did not miss a beat and, after 90 laps, I finally saw the chequered flag in the British Grand Prix at Aintree for the second time in my career. And it was my first time in a British car!'

Stirling was back at the Liverpool track to win the following year's Aintree 200 at the wheel of Rob Walker's F2 Cooper and then finished a strongly impressive second to Jack Brabham's works Cooper driving the front-engined BRM P25 in the 1959 British Grand Prix. After that, there would be only two more British Grands Prix held at Aintree, in 1961 and 1962.

The rain-soaked 1961 event delivered an impressive victory for Wolfgang von Trips at the wheel of the 'shark nose' Ferrari 156. This was one of two grand prix victories posted by the emergent German driver that season, which brought him to the very verge of the world championship before he was killed at Monza on the second lap of the Italian Grand Prix in a tragic collision with Jim Clark's Lotus 21. The accident also resulted in the death of more than a dozen onlookers crowded tightly against the spectator fencing.

Aintree's last shout came in 1962, when Jim Clark dominated the British Grand Prix in the iconic Lotus 25, qualifying on pole by a margin of half a second and then simply driving the opposition into the ground. Only three months had passed since Stirling Moss's F1 career had ended in the tangled wreckage of his Lotus 18/21 at Goodwood. And now the baton had passed to the emergent star of the next generation.

The atmosphere at Aintree seemed curious to those weaned on Silverstone and Brands Hatch, the horsey set perhaps feeling that it wasn't quite correct that such an obvious bastion of the Jockey Club's elitist influence should be invaded by high-octane, screaming, oil-leaking internal combustion engines.

One of my colleagues recalls that, in practice for the 1962 Aintree 200, Giancarlo Baghetti spun his Ferrari 156 into one of the Grand National jumps. Some short time later a cut-glass voice could be heard announcing, "Will Mr Giancarlo Baghetti come to the stewards' office as soon as possible." Baghetti complied, but if he expected any apology from the organiser for having left a potentially dangerous hazard in place, he was to be disappointed. Instead he received a formal dressing-down for damaging the infrastructure before, slightly baffled, he was allowed to return to his team.

By the start of the 1960s it was becoming clear that the owners of Brands Hatch were interested in expanding their circuit and maybe muscling in on the British Grand Prix business, but the Aintree management was too shrewd and canny to get sucked into an unpredictable Dutch auction to stage the UK's round of the world championship.

When Brands Hatch extended its track to full grand prix length, Mrs Topham concluded that it would be unprofitable to host the British Grand Prix at Aintree on what was likely to become a three-way basis and the full circuit at Aintree was closed in August 1964.

Motor racing thereafter was restricted to club events over a 1.64-mile shortened circuit and this continued until 1982. The track remains in existence to this day. But, wisely, the Aintree organisers got out of the grand prix business before costs spiralled dangerously out of control. The three-way option with their sharing the British Grand Prix with Brands Hatch and Silverstone on a rotating basis would never have worked.

Some observers have pointed to the fact that, since the inauguration of the official world championship in 1950, the French Grand Prix has taken place at Reims, Le Mans, Rouen-les-Essarts, Clermont Ferrand, Paul Ricard, Dijon-Prenois, and Magny-Cours, and asked why could not the British round of the title chase cast its net wider than just two circuits? The answer to that is simple: a succession of regional French government agencies fought each other single-mindedly in a bid to hold on to the race. That such a level of government support has not been available in the UK has become a major bone of contention over the years of negotiating for the future security of the British Grand Prix.

Brands Hatch, meanwhile, moved into the front line in negotiations to share the British Grand Prix with Silverstone. The Kentish circuit had first staged a motor race in 1950, although it had been used originally as a grass track for motorcycle events since before the war. Its location, in a natural bowl-shaped valley just off the A20 main road from London to Dover, was popular with spectators and eventually a cinder track was laid for the two-wheeled fraternity after the war, one of whom included a teenaged Bernard Charles Ecclestone. He would later also race a 500cc F3 Cooper-Norton at the track, which was only a few miles from his home and business base in Bexleyheath.

The 500 Club eventually helped, with a lobby of motorcycle racers, in raising the £17,000 required to lay an asphalt surface along the circuit's one-mile lap, which in those days was run anti-clockwise with the cars climbing up Paddock Bend to the left rather than plunging down it to the right.

The extension of the circuit from the bottom of Paddock Bend to the so-called Druids hairpin, and the switch to running events in a more conventional clockwise direction, was eventually completed in 1954. The first such race was won by Stuart Lewis-Evans in a Cooper-Norton at an average speed of 70.06mph. This may seem a rather modest pace on reflection, but the truth is that the track's facilities were pretty makeshift. At least the wicker fencing, which had previously lined the spectator areas, had now been replaced by protective earth banks. Protective for the onlookers, anyway.

Throughout the late 1950s Brands Hatch grew steadily and dramatically. It seemed to offer more of a 'show-biz' atmosphere for the paying public, something that Silverstone perhaps had yet to learn. Much of the driving force behind these initiatives came from John Webb, the track's forward-thinking publicity officer, who always seemed to have his antennae well tuned to pick up and capitalise on a worthwhile promotional opportunity.

Mixing mince pies and motor racing, for example, may have seemed something of an unlikely prospect, but Webb's astute judgement that a Boxing Day Brands meeting would be a success was absolutely vindicated and the fixture ran for many years in front of very reasonably sized crowds.

Yet it was at the end of the decade that things really took off for Brands Hatch. Early in 1960 planning permission was granted for an extension to the circuit. There was now a sharp left-hander at Kidney Bend, just behind the pits, leading out on to a long straight that then plunged into a high-speed dip, which led the cars to the fast up-hill right-hander at Hawthorn Hill.

Then it was right around Westfield, another plunge through Dingle Dell, and back through the left-hand Stirling's Bend, before a short straight brought the cars back to the original circuit at Clearways. At 2.65 miles in length, the enlarged Brands Hatch was a flowing high-speed track with plenty of challenges to keep competitors on their toes. As Maurice

Hamilton observed, "If ever a track was made for grand prix racing, then this was it."

Developing the new circuit would need considerable financial resources. The pits were now positioned between the start–finish and bottom straights, but it was clear that if Brands Hatch was going to make the F1 big time then it was going to need a complete revamp.

The key moment for Brands Hatch came in April 1961, when Grovewood Securities announced that it had acquired a controlling interest in Brands Hatch Circuit Ltd. From the moment that F1 cars first appeared on the lengthened track, it seemed pretty obvious to most of the motor racing fraternity that Brands Hatch would soon be bidding for a slice of the grand prix action.

John Webb was a key player in the emergence of Brands Hatch as a force within UK motor sport. He had been in and around motor racing since the early 1950s, not just at Brands Hatch but also organising some of the early charter flights to European grands prix under the banner of his Webbair charter company. A small spindly man who had a serious limp, Webb had a feel for what made a good business promotion when it came to judging the tastes of the paying customers.

When it was finally announced that the 1964 British Grand Prix would, after all, take place at Brands Hatch on 11 July there was much correspondence in the motor racing press about the relative merits of Brands Hatch and Silverstone, as well as the general lack of facilities for the paying spectator at British circuits. The feeling was that Grovewood was out to make 'big money' from the hapless spectators. It was probably fair to say that the sport had seen nothing yet.

Grovewood's response to this well-intentioned, and relatively mild, criticism was charmingly low key and civil. It drew attention to the fact that it was investing around £100,000 in the circuit, including the provision of additional spectator banks, the construction of what was billed as a 'modern 200-seater restaurant' behind the main grandstand, the upgrading of existing catering facilities, the addition of extra bars and cafeteria, and the construction of new toilet blocks.

These, it was pointed out with a degree of pride, would be 'all equipped with handbasins, towel machines and mirrors, and some of the ladies' toilets even have make-up tables.' Fancy!

In addition, much was made of the construction of the so-called Grovewood Suite, which, situated on the start–finish straight opposite the pits, was intended to provide first-class viewing for 'senior guests and distinguished visitors'. The paddock, however, was still on a steep slope and extremely makeshift by the standards of the day.

Again, Silverstone found itself having to share the British Grand Prix with another circuit, but now that Aintree had dropped out of the equation, the RAC decreed that henceforth the race would alternate regularly between the two established circuits. The 1964 race at Brands duly went ahead in cloudy and cool conditions with Jim Clark's Lotus 25B leading from start to finish to take the win by 2.8 seconds from Graham Hill's BRM P261, which had chased him all the way.

This was Clark's third British Grand Prix victory on the trot and meant he had been victorious at Aintree, Silverstone, and Brands Hatch in consecutive years. Clark would win again at Silverstone in 1965, making it four home grand prix wins in a row, and then add a final fifth success at Silverstone in 1967 less than a year before he was killed at Hockenheim.

Meanwhile, Silverstone would also have a new look for 1964. During the 1963 International Trophy meeting, Innes Ireland had highlighted some lingering safety concerns when he spun his BRP Lotus-BRM at high speed in a cloud of tyre smoke as he came through Woodcote corner. It was a luridly spectacular incident that sent many mechanics leaping on to the unprotected pit counter. On a lighter note, it was reported at the time that tape recorders in the vicinity were hurriedly switched off before they were fused by Ireland's comments as he fumbled for bottom gear and chased after the disappearing pack.

At the time, Ireland's wild moment seemed the sort of thing he might have laughed about – and probably did – in the beer tent after the race was over. But it had serious undertones. Concerns were mounting about the speed of cars through Woodcote and the safety of spectators on the outside and pit crews on the inside. Later that year, during a sports car race at the grand prix meeting, scrutineer Harold Cree was killed when he was hit by Christabel Carlisle's spinning Austin-Healey Sprite. The RAC immediately demanded that changes be made to the circuit layout. The result was a brand new pit lane separated from the main race track by a proper pit wall. The construction of this vital upgrade was completed in time for the 1965 British Grand Prix.

In autumn 1969 there was another crucial development that would help Silverstone as a business. Silverstone Circuits Ltd secured the freehold on a 42-acre tranche of the Silverstone estate, this being the area adjacent to the track itself. Now there seemed a very real chance of the club gaining ownership of the entire site, thereby decisively protecting Silverstone's motor racing future on an unchallenged, open-ended basis.

The final details took some time to hammer out, but at the BRDC's annual dinner in December 1970 club president the Hon. Gerald Lascelles announced that the freehold of another 398 acres had been completed and that the remainder, making 720 acres in all, was in prospect. By the end of 1971, the BRDC would own and operate the entire Silverstone estate and one did not need to be a mathematician to appreciate that staging the British Grand Prix would become its most significant commercial venture. Funding for this final land acquisition was hugely assisted by generous contributions from the loyal Beaverbrook Newspapers, GKN, Ford and Dunlop.

Title sponsorship reared its head for both the F1 events staged at Silverstone during 1971 in the form of the *Daily Express* GKN International Trophy and the Woolmark British Grand Prix. Cigarette advertising had long since found an outlet in F1, with the Gold Leaf Team Lotus tie-up, but very long-term trends were signalled during the year when Dr Roger Bannister, the first man to run a four-minute mile and the chairman of the Sports Council, called for a total ban on tobacco advertising at all sporting events. It was certainly a sign of things to come.

In the 1970 British Grand Prix at Brands Hatch, Jack Brabham looked as though he had got the upper hand in his battle for the lead against Jochen Rindt. Then, shortly before the finish, the Brabham BT33 began to cough and splutter because it was running low on fuel. Rindt swept past to victory and Ron Dennis, the future architect of the dominant multiple world championship-winning McLaren team, got the blame for not topping up the car sufficiently with fuel.

"I had to live with that reputation hanging around my neck for the best part of 40 years," Dennis says with a twinkle. "Then Nick Goozee, one of my colleagues at Brabham at the time – and who later went on to run the Penske Indycar team's UK base – wrote to me to apologise and admit that it was his fault after all. I knew I had topped up the car with all the necessary churns of fuel, but then he came along and changed the mixture settings to full rich."

It is a measure of Ron's deeply ingrained competitive streak that finally establishing the truth of what happened in the pit lane more than half a lifetime ago gives him a surge of satisfaction as well as a helping of ironic amusement. There was also a flip side to that particular coin in that, earlier that same season, Brabham had thrown away what seemed like a comfortable victory in the Monaco Grand Prix.

"Rindt was hunting Jack down in the closing stages, but there was no way he was going to catch Jack until he out-braked himself into the final hairpin – then called the Gasworks, but now Rascasse – and slid into the barrier. So everybody made mistakes, although I certainly didn't over that fuel issue."

The manner in which the dynamics of the relationship between Ecclestone and the circuits developed during the 1970s was instructive in the sense that, with hindsight, it is easy to see where it was going. But at the time there was a series of apparently isolated and unconnected episodes that were dismissed as all part of the cut and negotiating thrust of day-to-day F1 life. Threats were traded none too seriously and stand-offs were frequent.

By the start of the 1973 season, the Formula One Association, headed by Ecclestone, was holding firm to its demands for a dramatic increase in prize money guarantees and rumours began circulating that Indycars would be invited from the USA to flesh out the starting grid at several European races, including Silverstone.

It was an empty threat, of course, and the Americans never turned up – as surely they never intended to – but the fact remained that by the official closing date for British Grand Prix entries to be lodged – 8 June – only ten entries had been submitted, five of which were for F5000 machines. Not until 22 June, barely three weeks before the race's 14 July date, was the dispute finally settled and a three-year deal agreed.

"We know how much we'll be getting and they know how much it will cost them," said Ecclestone on behalf of the Formula One Association. It was another sign of how Ecclestone was using skill to edge his way towards supreme control of the commercial side of the F1 business.

The 1973 British Grand Prix is of course remembered for featuring one of the most spectacular multiple-car accidents in F1 history, leaving most competitors breathing a sigh of relief that the pit lane was now safely separated from the main circuit proper.

The fight for the world championship was developing into a three-way battle between Tyrrell legend Jackie Stewart – who, unbeknown to all but a handful of his nearest and dearest, had decided to retire at the end of the year – and the JPS Lotus 72 twins Emerson Fittipaldi and Ronnie Peterson. At this race Peterson took pole from the McLaren M23s of Denny Hulme and Peter Revson, but all eyes were on the third row of the grid, where Jody Scheckter, the mercurial South African rising star who was driving a third McLaren, was out to make his name.

Scheckter made a terrific start and was in fourth place as the pack flashed under the bridge into Woodcote at the end of the opening lap. Hulme, running third, glanced in his mirror, reckoned Jody was coming up on him far too quickly, and gave the headstrong novice room to slip past into third.

Denny was absolutely right in his judgement: Scheckter was carrying far too much speed. As he hurtled around Woodcote, his McLaren ran wide on to the grass and spun back across the track into the pit wall, triggering a pile-up that eliminated nine cars from the grid. The race was stopped just as Stewart led the pack through to complete his second lap, and later restarted only after Italian Andrea de Adamich was cut from the crumpled wreckage of his Brabham. Mercifully, there was no fire.

There were more changes for Silverstone in the pipeline towards the end of 1974. All winter testing was shelved so that work on the new £120,000 pit complex could be completed in time for the following season. It featured no fewer than 44 garages and a much wider pit lane, and the pit lane exit road was modified so it merged in with the circuit again beyond the apex of Copse corner.

As it turned out, there were also some safety modifications to be made in time for the 1975 British Grand Prix. Niki Lauda's split-second victory in the Ferrari 312T over Emerson Fittipaldi's McLaren on the last corner of the non-title International Trophy race in April that year would mark the final major event for which Woodcote was used in all its unfettered high-speed glory.

Spectator safety had again vaulted to the head of the F1 agenda after the Spanish Grand Prix at Barcelona's Montjuïc Park circuit early in the year. After suffering a rear-wing failure as it crested the rise beyond the pits, Rolf Stommelen's Hill-

Cosworth vaulted the guard rail, killing five onlookers. The Grand Prix Drivers' Association (GPDA) immediately initiated a series of circuit inspections and when 1972 Monaco Grand Prix winner Jean-Pierre Beltoise arrived at Silverstone he was quick to voice his concern over the very limited run-off area on the outside of Woodcote.

As a direct result of this, Emerson Fittipaldi and Jody Scheckter briefly tried a makeshift chicane layout at Woodcote during a break in official pre-event tyre testing in preparation for the British Grand Prix. It was adopted for the race, even though its presence was not welcomed by all the fans who had bought tickets in the grandstand adjacent to this point on the circuit. But at the end of the day it was a prudent development and at least ensured that nobody ended up with a Tyrrell in their lap.

"You have to realise that FIA regulations demand that fencing will restrain a wayward car if it leaves the track at 30 degrees at high speed," said Ecclestone. "You only have to think about what sort of fencing would be needed at Woodcote to realise that spectators would not be able to see through it."

Yet one might be forgiven for concluding that Brands Hatch was doing little better during the mid-1970s when it came to the challenge of administering the British Grand Prix and moving the event on to another level in terms of public facilities and slick presentation. In fact, the truth of the matter was that Silverstone was being the more proactive of the two by 1974, the year in which James Hunt's Hesketh 308 memorably won the BRDC International Trophy event at the Northamptonshire circuit.

Granted, the 1973 British Grand Prix had been badly disrupted by the multiple-car accident, but that had hardly been the fault of the promoters. By the time the 1974 season dawned, although a winter of economic depression and three-day weeks could still be seen in Britain's collective rear-view mirror, Brands was, to put it mildly, looking run-down and frankly a grotty dump that screamed out for more investment on the part of its owner Grovewood Securities.

Anybody attending the 1974 Race of Champions will have been appalled by the state of the public car parks. True enough, the torrential conditions provided a wonderful backdrop against which the veteran Jacky Ickx drove his works Lotus 72 with consummate flair to score a great victory, running around the outside of Niki Lauda's Ferrari at Paddock Bend to take the lead before pulling away.

Such genius behind the wheel may well have warmed the frozen cockles of any race fan's heart, but I well recall spending over four hours attempting to extricate my Triumph TR6 from the main car park behind the start-line straight. Okay, it's easy to look back on that period through rose-tinted spectacles, but, in truth, you can quite see why Bernie Ecclestone got so exasperated with F1.

He was trying to raise the bar and improve standards, while too many race promoters were continuing to present their customers with an unwelcome automotive equivalent of an Outward Bound course on the somewhat fragile premise that 'this is what it has always been like'. The RAC, as the sport's administrator, could also at that time be considered implicated in this chaotic state of affairs, as events at the 1974 and 1976 British Grands Prix amply testified.

Brands Hatch looked more-than-usually dusted, rutted, and ill-kempt when the time arrived for the 1974 British Grand Prix.

It looked as though the race would turn out to be a piece of cake for Niki Lauda and his Ferrari 312B3, the Austrian qualifying comfortably on pole position and pulling away steadily from Jody Scheckter's Tyrrell 007 from the very first corner.

Lauda seemed well in control for much of the distance, but about 20 laps from the chequered flag, Niki could tell that something was going wrong with his car. The right rear tyre had picked up a slow puncture and Niki could feel the car sliding more, generally feeling "looser", as he negotiated the many left-hand corners. The dilemma was plain. Niki now had to decide whether he would stop to change the tyre or plod on in the hope that the Goodyear rubber would hold together until the end.

Doggedly, he pressed on, but the Ferrari's lap times were gradually lengthening. First Scheckter surged by and into the lead, followed soon after by Emerson Fittipaldi's McLaren into second place. Then Niki's tyre flew apart and, with just one lap to go, he tore into the pit lane, where a replacement was fitted and he was quickly accelerating away.

What faced Lauda when he reached the end of the pit lane was simply unbelievable. The exit had been roped off and an official had parked a Ford Cortina diagonally across what was technically the racing line. Contemptuously, an official just shook his arms dismissively as Lauda approached. There was nothing left for Niki to do but switch off, release his seat harness, and climb out. He was close to tears.

Quite rightly, Ferrari's new team manager Luca di Montezemolo was not minded to leave matters there. He protested to the RAC stewards and received a flat rejection. Ferrari then appealed to the FIA, which took eight hours to deliberate on the matter a week or so later, reinstating Niki to fifth place, which is where he would have finished had he just been permitted to drive another 20 feet or so and properly exit the pits, triggering the timing line as he did so. It had been a truly nonsensical turn of events.

To be fair to Brands Hatch, things had improved considerably by the 1976 British Grand Prix. The track owners had spent £300,000 expanding the paddock and re-profiling Cooper Straight, the section of track just behind it, to accommodate those modifications. Paddock Bend had also been realigned slightly and given a run-off area worth the name, a development that most F1 drivers who had been regulars at Brands Hatch over the years considered to be long overdue.

The infrastructure may have moved on, but the RAC officials seemed no more capable of administering the event properly than they had been two years earlier. In fact, the 1976 British Grand Prix turned out to be one of the event's biggest fiascos in living memory.

Lauda qualified his Ferrari 312T2 on pole position, opting for the 'up-camber' left-hand position on the front row of the starting grid with James Hunt's McLaren M23 lining up to his right. Hunt was slow off the mark, allowing Clay Regazzoni's Ferrari to burst through from the second row of the grid to hound Lauda going into Paddock Bend for the first time.

Regazzoni, free spirit as always, collided with Lauda and spun as they went into the corner. Hunt tried to go through on the left, but Regazzoni's Ferrari was by this time rolling backwards to the outside of the turn and James clipped Clay's right rear wheel with his right front, vaulting the McLaren high up into the air.

James was winded by the impact as his McLaren came crashing down again on all four wheels and, reasoning his race was over after seeing crossed yellow and oil flags as he motored gently up the hill to Druids, prepared to pull up behind the pits on Cooper Straight. At least, that's how James explained it officially. It would be ungallant to suggest that this was not quite the case, particularly as Hunt is no longer here to defend his own corner, but a colleague of mine who spoke to James the moment he pulled up behind the pits said that James was surprised to see a red flag being waved at the start line and could hardly contain his apparent astonishment that the race was being stopped.

After endless argument between Ferrari, McLaren, and RAC officials, against a backdrop of noisy jeering and barracking from the huge crowd of pro-Hunt supporters in the grandstands all around the circuit, the race was restarted over its entire distance with Hunt back in his original starting position in his repaired machine.

Lauda led comfortably from the second start of the afternoon, with James initially trailing by a few seconds. But as the cars laid a veneer of additional rubber on the racing line, Hunt found his McLaren's grip improving literally by the lap. Within a few laps he was closing the gap to the leading Ferrari and on lap 45 he dived audaciously down the inside of his old friend into the Druids hairpin, thereafter surging away to win commandingly. And frustratingly. James later said he was disappointed at the way in which Niki effectively capitulated once he had been overtaken.

The Englishman had wanted to win a close wheel-to-wheel fight, but Lauda would not oblige. The master tactician, Niki not only knew well when he was beaten, but probably also realised that Hunt's victory would not stand even though the RAC stewards had rejected the Ferrari protest that Hunt was not still running when the race was stopped and therefore was not eligible to take the restart.

So, for the second time in three years, the British Grand Prix ended with Ferrari appealing to the FIA – and winning its case. Many weeks after being cheered to the echo by his loyal supporters, Hunt was disqualified from his win at Brands Hatch. This would dramatically tighten the championship battle at the head of the points table, a contest that would eventually be won by James by a single point from his season-long adversary, who had missed the Austrian and Dutch Grands Prix after suffering fearful burns in a fiery crash on the first lap of the German Grand Prix at the Nürburgring.

Curiously, Hunt never warmed to Silverstone, even though it had been the venue at which he laid the foundations for his 1976 title challenge, including his fourth place in the 1973 British Grand Prix driving the Hesketh March and then victory in the following year's International Trophy meeting.

James made no bones about it. He found Brands Hatch more involving, recalling the feeling of contact with the huge crowd as he swept around Clearways for the last time coming up to take the chequered flag in 1976. He said he felt as though he could have reached from the cockpit of his McLaren M23 and touched them. At Silverstone the fans were too distant, he felt.

Victory there in the 1977 British Grand Prix at the wheel of the unloved McLaren M26 went no way to changing those feelings. "After winning at Brands the previous year, that 1977 result just does not begin to compare in any way, shape, or form," he told Maurice Hamilton. "I have always felt that Silverstone was as dull as ditch water from a driver's point of view. Okay, it's reasonably challenging because of the quick corners but it has no character, no atmosphere, because the crowd are more spread out."

In 1978 the British Grand Prix was back at Brands Hatch, by which time it was becoming clear that James Hunt's appetite for F1 had almost run its course. Two years had passed since he won his world championship and the development of McLaren's latest M26 had proved something of a disappointment. Moreover, Hunt was now so nervous that he was regularly throwing up before getting into his car for the start of the race and was chain smoking not just cigarettes. After only a handful of laps he spun on Bottom Straight, mowed down a corner marker, and shuddered to a halt. No other car was involved.

The Brands Hatch regulars, meanwhile, may have recalled Clay Regazzoni as the man who indirectly wiped out James's prospects of winning the 1976 race, but in 1979 the moustachioed Swiss also went down in history as the man who posted the Williams team's maiden grand prix victory in the British Grand Prix at Silverstone.

Alan Jones's Williams FW07 dominated the race from the start, but a cracked water pump casting caused his car's Cosworth V8 engine to expire in a cloud of smoke and steam. On the pit wall, Frank Williams glanced fleetingly at the stricken machine as it rolled into the pit lane before switching his gaze back to the track, where Regazzoni was now equally well in command. Williams commercial director Sheridan Thynne cited this as an example of Frank's ability to pay zero attention to something that was not the absolute priority of the moment.

Jones was out, so Clay's survival was now the most important thing on his mind.

As Regazzoni's Williams FW07 clicked off those final miles to the chequered flag, a huge wave of patriotic fervour understandably seemed to envelop the enthusiastic crowd. Perhaps for the first time, Frank would appreciate how much support and respect he had from the ordinary race fans, who seemed genuinely delighted that this outsider who'd struggled against the odds for so many years had at last made the big time. It was as if Southend United had dragged themselves into the premier league and were now poised to win the Cup Final.

Suddenly it was over. Clay roared through the long Woodcote right-hander to cross the finishing line and the Williams personnel chased down the pit lane towards the podium, literally whooping with delight. Frank walked a little way behind them, his face flickering with an almost self-conscious grin. His team had done it. What once had been perceived as a ragbag of F1 also-rans had now scaled a significant, unbelievable peak. It seemed as though Frank could hardly take it all in, as though he wanted to stand still and allow himself to be swept away in the vortex of this unbridled emotion that had erupted all around him.

CHAPTER THREE

A CHALLENGE TO THE
STATUS QUO

Ironically Brands Hatch was the oldest and longest-established of the motor racing venues to stage the British Grand Prix. Its story began in the immediate pre-war years, when it was a makeshift grass track racing venue, but it was a long road through to the 1960s when it first staged a world championship F1 race. Twenty years later, its F1 days seemed to be over.

Brands Hatch alternated smoothly with Silverstone as the home of the British Grand Prix from 1964 to 1986, thriving largely thanks to the entrepreneurial skill and foresight of John Webb, who had risen to become the managing director of its owner, Motor Circuit Developments (MCD).

The 1961 sale of MCD to Grovewood Securities was effectively masterminded by Webb and his success in so doing earned him a place on the board of the parent company. Nine years later, in 1972, Grovewood Securities would be taken over by Eagle Star Holdings, which in turn was purchased by British American Tobacco (BAT) in the early 1980s. But by 1985 BAT, ironically considering that just over a decade later it would be back in F1 as a team owner backing Craig Pollock's new team built around Jacques Villeneuve, decided that motor racing no longer seriously meshed with its wide investment interests and began looking for a buyer.

Webb could see his opportunity here. He contacted Patrick

Sheahy, the chairman of BAT, setting out his stall with the crystal clear request that he would like to be granted the first option to purchase should Grovewood's motor racing interests finally come up for sale. Webb was now running MCD with his wife Angela, who had risen to the post of deputy managing director in the early 1980s. He was playing for high stakes. There was much manoeuvring behind the F1 scenes to ensure that each country had a single, designated circuit on which to host its round of the world championship, so whoever won this particular battle could look forward to potentially high earning capacity in the future. And, as things transpired, a great deal of cost if they wanted to keep up with the ever-higher standards that Bernie Ecclestone would require from F1 circuits in the future.

Of course, finding somebody with sufficiently deep pockets to bankroll the Webbs' buy-out plan would not be the work of a moment. Their bottom-line interest was to beat Silverstone to that crock of gold at the end of the rainbow that was the permanent, ongoing contract to stage the British Grand Prix at Brands Hatch. Practical considerations, such as whether it would really be possible to continue upgrading the Kent track so that it would keep pace with standards elsewhere, were more problematic.

By February 1986, the Webbs had targeted two potential investors. One was John Foulston, the millionaire founder of the Atlantic Computers computer-leasing company. He was a keen amateur racer with the bank balance necessary to indulge his preference for famous and exotic racing cars. The other potentially interested bidder was Bernie Ecclestone.

According to Terry Lovell's fascinating book *Bernie Ecclestone:*

King of Sport, Bernie, Foulston, and the Webbs met in early spring 1986 to begin preliminary talks that might lead to a deal. Foulston and Ecclestone would go 50-50 in a deal to purchase the Brands Hatch freehold while the Webbs would assume a 20 per cent share of the operational company Brands Hatch Circuit Ltd. Both the Webbs and Foulston seemed confident that a deal could be done for a price tag of around £3.5 million, which included the circuits at Oulton Park and Snetterton as well as Brands itself.

Yet perhaps the Foulstons and the Webbs had not done their homework as carefully as they might have thought. One lesson of history was that Bernie was not generally one for partners; if he wanted to buy a business *he* wanted to buy that business and that meant controlling it exclusively. Ron Tauranac had learned that lesson back in 1971 when he had enquired whether Ecclestone had any interest in becoming a partner in the ownership of the Brabham F1 team. Bernie said no, but instead agreed to buy 100 per cent of the team.

Ecclestone eventually backed out of the deal to go halves with Foulston. Things seemed about to change. On 18 May 1986, a press conference was convened in the Grovewood Suite at Brands Hatch, at which Webb announced proudly that John Foulston, the mega-wealthy and successful owner of Atlantic Computers, had just purchased Brands Hatch, Oulton Park, and Snetterton from Eagle Star Holdings, the parent company of Grovewood Securities, for £5.25 million.

The price hike to that eventual figure from its originally estimated level of £3.5 million was in part due to a late expression of interest from British Car Auctions founder David Wickens, who thought that there was a possibility of the facilities at Brands Hatch offering potential for expanding his existing business interests without interfering with the racing.

One week later Bernie Ecclestone, on behalf of the Formula One Constructors' Association (FOCA), announced that a deal had been signed to guarantee Silverstone the British Grand Prix for the next five years. FISA, the sporting arm of the FIA, had said that it wanted each country to have a designated track for its national grand prix and Silverstone had been chosen because it was believed to have greater scope for development.

"Silverstone has undertaken to build a totally new pit complex, expand the paddock, and complete long-term improvements which will really make it the centre of British motor racing," said Ecclestone. It was a refrain that, while welcome at the time, would be heard in a subtly less charitable context from time to time over the years that followed, depending on the state of Ecclestone's relationship with Silverstone's owners.

This decision to commit to Silverstone was announced officially by Jean-Marie Balestre, the president of FISA, during the Belgian Grand Prix at Spa-Francorchamps on 24 May. Maurice Hamilton, then the motor racing correspondent of *The Guardian*, relayed the information to the Webbs in a telephone call from Belgium. They were stunned, although they quickly regained their composure for public consumption. In terms of negotiating pizzazz, this had been vintage Ecclestone: keep both sides guessing, keep all your options open until the very last moment, and always be ready to alter your position if something more expedient and profitable comes up.

Reassured by the commercial stability engendered by the new long-term deal to stage the British Grand Prix, Silverstone confirmed that it was investing £1 million on new developments for 1987, including the reprofiled Woodcote corner, an access tunnel at Copse corner, and 40 new pit garages. The revised Woodcote complex was readied in time for the pre-season F1 test session scheduled for 2 April.

The circuit alterations had slowed average lap speeds since 1985, when Keke Rosberg had planted his Williams-Honda FW10 turbo on pole position at an average speed of just on 160mph, but during tyre testing before the grand prix Nigel Mansell still averaged 154mph. "The new corner will be much better once it has got some rubber down," he stressed.

Shortly before the main race of the year, Bernie Ecclestone firmly rebuffed continued speculation and stressed that F1 fully intended to honour its five-year contract with Silverstone, even though the RAC Motor Sports Association supported a bid from Brands Hatch to hold the grand prix in 1988.

By the time FISA finally put the matter beyond doubt in favour of Silverstone, it was December 1987 and further developments were in hand, including new debris fencing, a bigger media centre, and further improved spectator facilities. 'Beyond doubt', that is, as far as anything can be beyond doubt in the F1 business.

The amount of upgrading and general development work completed at both major British circuits over the years not only sent a signal as to just how costly a sustained programme to retain the grand prix might become over a much longer period, but also served as a reminder of just how high the required standards would become as F1 expanded to new venues, many of them without a long-established motor racing heritage, during the frenzied expansion of the sport in the decades to come.

Yet there were aspects of Ecclestone's relationship with

Silverstone that were less confrontational and much more sympathetic. The 1988 season marked Silverstone's 40th anniversary, but that important event was saddened by the death of Jimmy Brown, who had been the first track manager back in 1948 and by the time of his death was the chairman of Silverstone Circuits Ltd. When Bernie opened the new press facilities at Silverstone on the Thursday before the 1988 British Grand Prix, he was joined by Jimmy's widow Kay as he officially named the new building the Jimmy Brown Centre.

Bernie was in a notably good mood on this occasion and delivered a few words of appreciation for Jimmy's contribution to Silverstone's success. He was then approached by BRDC secretary Pierre Aumonier, who handed him a thick brown envelope containing honorary membership of the club. Those present felt that Bernie was genuinely touched by this gesture.

Later, Bernie would attend the club's extraordinary general meeting, where he would stand up and make an offer of help, even financial assistance, to the BRDC, at which point – in a supremely ill-judged move – one member, now no longer alive, shouted "We don't want your money" (or words to that effect).

Soon afterwards, track manager Brian Pallett drove Bernie to his waiting helicopter for his flight back to London. Pallett, ashen-faced, returned to the meeting to confide, "Bernie was furious. He was already at about 3,000ft by the time he got into the helicopter. He could have flown back to London without it."

There, in a nutshell, you had the essence of the problem. Ecclestone and the BRDC were both passionate about the sport in their very different ways, but philosophically their interests sometimes seemed irreconcilable. Adding extra layers of tension and unease to the veneer of this relationship would be as much a continuing problem as the actual mathematics involved in balancing the books for the British Grand Prix itself.

Meanwhile, elsewhere in the sport's upper reaches, Jean-Marie Balestre was re-elected as FISA president for another four years and many people felt it was a sign of how much closer the relationship between FOCA and FISA had become that Bernie Ecclestone had stepped up to take responsibility for the FIA's commercial affairs.

Balestre hailed his new colleague as a "redoubtable businessman" and, as a symbol in this supposed new era of cooperation, a new Concorde Agreement was signed to carry F1 through to 1991. With the benefit of hindsight, of course, it can now be seen as the thin end of the wedge.

By the mid-1980s, Bernie Ecclestone was firmly in control of the F1 business. Relentless and always pushing, pushing, pushing. Whether it was a question of how the F1 paddock was laid out or whether a sponsorship decal was slightly out of line on the rear-wing end plate of one of his immaculately turned-out Brabham F1 cars, the best was only just good enough for Ecclestone. Everything he did, one felt, was only a stopping place on the journey to the next big thing, the next towering achievement. And his ambitions were not to be denied or even deflected.

The 1987 British Grand Prix was a truly memorable classic event by any standards. The Williams-Honda FW11Bs of Nigel Mansell and Nelson Piquet were in an absolute class of their own, but Piquet found himself dramatically wrong-footed in the race when it came to getting the gloves off in a close tussle with Mansell.

The Englishman always seemed to be able to dig deep into

his resources of bravery and determination when it came to performing in front of his passionately vociferous home crowd and 1987 was no exception at Silverstone. Between them, the two Williams drivers delivered a tour de force that seriously underlined just what a magnificent track this really was.

Brands Hatch now seemed as though it had been very seriously left out in the cold.

There was another chunk of irony associated with this potential development. At that time, it was one of motor sport's most enduring legends that John Foulston fell out with Ecclestone and the British Grand Prix was lost to the Kent circuit as a direct result.

"Yes, I've heard that story, too," Nicola Foulston told me with an airy insouciance during 1999. "But I don't know the real truth of it." Was she being coy, or did she really not know the background to these stories? Either way, it was a curiously coquettish response, I felt. Because, as we would subsequently discover, there was more than a sliver of truth in that particular story.

CHAPTER FOUR

Brands Hatch
Makes its Bid

How the gloves came off in what was to become a protracted, tense, and bitter contest for control of Britain's round of the F1 world championship. The battle lines were drawn between what was perceived as the establishment at Silverstone and the new entrepreneurs at Brands Hatch. It would be a hard slog.

After the death of Atlantic Computers tycoon John Foulston, when he crashed his Offenhauser-engined McLaren M15 Indycar testing at Silverstone in 1987, his wife Mary inherited control of Brands Hatch, which had been owned by her family. Their daughter Nicola was barely out of her teens at that time, but was already a chip off the old block and would soon take over the running of the family's motor racing empire. She would make a bid to Bernie Ecclestone for the British Grand Prix contract. And be successful. But that was the best part of a decade down the track and there was plenty of drama to occupy the minds of Silverstone's owners as the intervening years unfolded.

So the 1990s rolled by with the nerve-racking frisson of uncertainty, which negotiating with Ecclestone always engendered, continuing on each occasion the grand prix contract came up for renewal. Financing was always marginal for Silverstone when it came to hosting Britain's round of the world championship, but in 1992 the BRDC board made a strategic error of deeply worrying proportions while attempting to pursue a strategy to ensure the race's future through the next round of contract negotiations.

The focal point of the BRDC board's concern was another dig in the ribs from Ecclestone, which was interpreted as another strong hint that if Silverstone didn't continue investing in its infrastructure, well, its days could be numbered.

Stampeded into what turned out to be an intemperate course of action, the board, led by club president Jack Sears, brokered a deal whereby Silverstone would purchase a stake in the retail motor sales group owned by Tom Walkinshaw's TWR organisation.

Walkinshaw, no mean driver himself in the 1970s and 1980s, was also a hard-nosed business operator and a salesman of the highest order. Hindsight is a wonderful thing, but the way the board justified to the members what looked like a panic-stricken deal seems both naive and extraordinary. In equal measure.

Jack Sears, a pleasant and well-respected member of the motor racing establishment, issued a statement to the members. 'Steps have been taken to safeguard the future of Silverstone as Britain's premier motor racing venue,' he explained. 'A new joint venture between Silverstone Circuits and the TWR Group has been formed. The new company is the Silverstone Motor Group Limited and the investment represents another commercial coup made by the directors of the BRDC and Silverstone Circuits on your behalf.'

Sears continued, 'This particular business venture, one of several successfully completed by the BRDC over the years, has recently become the subject of much speculation and rumour amongst club members. I would like to take this opportunity to say that your representatives on both boards at all times acted properly and in the interests of the BRDC and Silverstone Circuits Limited.

'The boards are charged by the membership to manage the business of the club – an increasingly demanding task in the highly competitive and commercial world of motor racing. I believe your board has discharged its role in a highly professional and businesslike manner over the years and the current success of Silverstone is testament to that. Furthermore, I have every confidence that, under the present directors, the BRDC will continue to flourish as the most respected and prestigious motor racing club in the world.'

Summarising the deal with Walkinshaw, who was then himself chairman of Silverstone Circuits Ltd, Sears stated, 'As your club president I personally recommend you vote in favour of the joint venture and support board directors who have worked tirelessly on your behalf over the years to run a highly successful club and motor racing circuit.

'It is my belief that voting against your board will place the future of your club, the circuit and the British Grand Prix at great risk.'

Walkinshaw had clearly done one hell of a sales pitch.

The origins of the deal went back to the end of 1991, when the Silverstone board became aware that the TWR garage group was restructuring and that part of that plan was to seek outside investors or partners. The BRDC board decided that such a business partnership might be worthy of investigation. The astonishing fact that these negotiations were conducted without the membership being advised in advance would return to haunt some members of the BRDC board in court some months later.

So what did the BRDC board believe would be the advantages of all this? Increased sites for circuit ticket sales, outlets for Silverstone Leisurewear merchandise, increased opportunities to sell corporate hospitality to fleet buyers, and access to a 10,000-name marketing database were all touted as possible areas of development.

The franchise sites involved were at Oxford, Solihull, Coventry, Gerrards Cross and St Albans, and the automotive brands involved included Jaguar, Land Rover, BMW, Porsche, Nissan, Mazda and Citroën. On the face of it, the proposal looked tempting for Silverstone, at least at first glance.

The briefing document continued to say that 'Tom Walkinshaw's directorships might have caused a conflict of interests but he declared his interests and took no part in voting on any aspect of the matter at Silverstone or BRDC board meetings.

'Throughout the investigations and discussions, Tom Walkinshaw's proven track record and standing in the motor industry and motor sport was a constant reminder that not only would Silverstone's partner in the joint venture share common interests, but it would also bring management flair and dynamism to the enterprise.

'In approving the joint venture, the board recognised that advantage had to be taken of the window of opportunity that existed in the UK motor industry. This view was supported by the findings of independent City analysts and market forecasts.

'Investment in the joint venture will help the necessary funds to be generated within the time scale available and provide a significant number of marketing opportunities for Silverstone.'

The BRDC board had clearly been jogged into precipitate action by what it perhaps erroneously felt was a direct and very specific threat to its circuit.

"Silverstone is a famous old place with great traditions like Monza," Ecclestone mused. "But it, like Britain, has no divine right to a grand prix. It is up to Tom Walkinshaw and Silverstone to do something about it themselves – they've got to keep their promise to continue developing the circuit."

Throughout the whole episode the recurring theme from the board in general, and Jack Sears in particular, was that, 'Having taken financial and legal advice, the Silverstone board satisfied itself that a joint venture with the TWR garage group was indeed a sound business proposition.' So far so good, but there was plenty of 'PR fluff' involved in the presentation, too.

Consider this: 'The company would also be in the best possible position to maximise the business synergy and tangible and intangible benefits...' and so on.

Though both had been very successful racing drivers, Jack Sears and Tom Walkinshaw could hardly have been cut from more different cloth.

Sears won the first official British touring car championship in 1958 at the wheel of an Austin Westminster. He would later earn a reputation as a highly respected sports car racer and memorably won the 1964 British Grand Prix supporting race at Brands Hatch at the wheel of a Willment team AC Cobra despite being flagged into the pits for a penalty and having to climb back through the field to take the win. Photographs of Sears shaking his fist at race officials as he accelerated back into the race were regarded as amazing by those who were well acquainted with the mild-mannered farmer from rural Norfolk.

ABOVE: *The way we were, with straw bales on the edge of the Silverstone perimeter road delineating the makeshift circuit before the start of the official World Championship in 1950.* (LAT)

BELOW: *Not quite the Paddock Club, but a huge occasion nonetheless. King George VI, Queen Elizabeth and the Princesses, Elizabeth and Margaret, were enthusiastic spectators at the 1950 British GP.* (LAT)

ABOVE: *Froilan Gonzalez sprints away from the front row of the grid at the start of the 1954 British GP at Silverstone, leaving the Mercedes W196 streamliners to be swallowed up by the rest of the pack.* (LAT)

BELOW: *It would be different the following year at Aintree when Stirling Moss scored a close victory ahead of team-mate Juan Manuel Fangio, heading a Mercedes 1-2-3-4 grand slam.* (Mercedes)

ABOVE: *Jim Clark won four straight British GP victories between 1962 and 65, respectively at Aintree, Silverstone, Brands Hatch and Silverstone again – and then a fifth in 1967! Here his Lotus 25, the quintessential 1960s F1 machine, shaves the inside wall at Copse on the way to his '63 success.* (LAT)

BELOW: *The Lotus is loaded onto an articulated truck for his victory lap of the circuit.* (LAT)

ABOVE & BELOW: *Jackie Stewart was a pivotal Silverstone personality during his successful racing career and later worked tirelessly in his role as president of the British Racing Drivers' Club. He is seen heading to victory in the 1969 British GP (above) at the wheel of the Tyrrell-entered Matra MS80 and two years later (below) repeating the achievement in Tyrrell 003.* (LAT)

ABOVE: *The opening lap of the 1977 British GP saw James Hunt's McLaren M26 and John Watson's Brabham BT45B wheel-to-wheel for the lead. Hunt won on this occasion after 'Wattie' was delayed by fuel feed trouble.* (LAT)

BELOW: *But the Ulsterman eventually emerged victorious in 1981 when he scored the first win for the Ron Dennis-run McLaren International squad.* (LAT)

OVERLEAF: *A panoramic view of Silverstone in all its glory.* (Sutton Motorsport Images)

ABOVE: *Mansell mania was an integral part of the British GP in the mid 1980s and early 1990s with Nigel winning three times at Silverstone and once at Brands Hatch.* (Sutton Motorsport Images)

BELOW: *The British driver's Williams FW14B is mobbed as the crowds spilled onto the track after his final Silverstone victory in 1992.* (Sutton Motorsport Images)

By contrast, Walkinshaw was a tough and gritty Scot who came from a farming family near Prestonpans, on the banks of the Firth of Forth to the east of Edinburgh. After trying to make his mark as a single-seater driver, Tom thrived as an international touring car ace, ironically scoring one of the best victories of his career when he shared the winning BMW CSL coupé with John Fitzpatrick in the 1976 Silverstone six-hour endurance event, the pair of them fending off the second-placed Porsche to take the chequered flag by little more than the length of the Woodcote chicane.

But Walkinshaw at that stage in his career was a sharp businessman with a shrewd eye for a deal. During the early 1970s he had come to recognise that he had a happy knack for test and development work. His reputation in this sphere had grown to the point at which many private owners were only too happy to pay him a daily fee to sort out their own saloon racers.

Walkinshaw would later prepare the 5.3-litre Jaguar XJS coupés that he would drive to victory in the 1984 European touring car championship, which acted as a springboard to the development of a succession of Group C Jaguar sports cars that would win the world sports car championship in 1987 and Le Mans the following year.

He would later become involved with the Benetton F1 team and was close to the centre of the controversy that loomed in 1994 after Michael Schumacher's title-winning B194 was found to be equipped with an illegal electronic control system, although the governing body effectively accepted the team's assurance that the software controlling this system had been disarmed and the 'best evidence' was that it had not been used during any of that season's races.

It did not take long for the BRDC board to find itself in hot water with its membership for agreeing the Walkinshaw deal behind closed doors. It emerged that the club's legal advisers were wrong in telling their clients that UK company law did not demand that the membership vote on such a course of business action.

A stormy annual general meeting revealed the strength of resistance to the BRDC's board decision. Members were horrified to discover the realities of the situation, which was made even worse by the fact that the board refused to tell the membership precisely how much had been paid for the 50 per cent stake in Walkinshaw's motor business. Two months later an extraordinary general meeting was convened, ostensibly to gain approval from the members and at which it finally emerged that the sum invested was a stunning £5.3 million. The board sought the members' approval. Which was refused.

The club's solicitors' failure to advise the board that the prior approval of the voting members would be a legal requirement to validate the contract caused a huge row. When the agreement was placed before the members in the vain hope that they would retrospectively legitimise it, the directors instead found themselves instructed to extricate the club from its commitment immediately.

The membership really did have a strong adverse reaction to the prospect of doing business with Walkinshaw's companies. Ken Tyrrell and Innes Ireland, in particular, admitted that they were extremely alarmed. They could not understand why the club was investing in the motor trade, with which it had no previous connection, in the middle of a recession. This concern was mirrored by many other members, including Martin Colvill, Tommy Sopwith and Frank Sytner, who had considerable experience in the retail motor business and joined Tyrrell and Ireland in organising pressure for a review.

There followed a most acrimonious period in the BRDC's history, which eventually resulted, following a period of litigation, in Walkinshaw repurchasing the shares, albeit at a substantially reduced price. That deal became unconditional on 22 April 1994, when it was approved by the membership of the BRDC. Needless to say, the club's board was replaced in totality as a result of this error in commercial judgement.

On 21 December 1992 a writ was issued by the BRDC's lawyers against Tom Walkinshaw and TWR and against those directors of the BRDC and Silverstone Circuits who had formed part of the working group.

The tortured issue dragged on through 1993. It was impossible not to have some sympathy with those BRDC and Silverstone Circuits directors who had seemingly blundered into this legal minefield after acting with the best intentions, in their minds, for the club's future interests and for Silverstone's.

As one mentioned to me, "It was a sobering and deeply upsetting position to be in, not only to be regarded as somehow now being outcasts amongst people who had been friends for many years and also perhaps faced with the possibility of being bankrupted and even losing our homes."

Negotiations with Walkinshaw limped on through summer 1993, during which he proposed repurchasing the shares on condition that a new company to be formed by him would be granted a 15-year lease of Silverstone circuit. An extraordinary general meeting was convened and his suggestion rejected.

Towards the end of 1993 Denys Rohan was appointed chief executive of Silverstone Circuits. Rohan was a chartered accountant and had a background both in professional accountancy and as a senior executive of major companies in the retail car trade. He met Walkinshaw on 2 December 1993 and started negotiations that eventually settled the whole vexed issue once and for all.

The essence of the settlement was that Walkinshaw, or his nominee company, would acquire Silverstone Circuits' shares in the Silverstone Motor Group for a total of £3.2 million, while the BRDC and Silverstone Circuits regained control over the Silverstone name and logo. It was also agreed that the main parties were to pay their own costs.

The BRDC and Silverstone Circuits made a contribution of £120,000 and Walkinshaw £50,000 to the directors' costs. At the end of the day, the BRDC's costs in pursuing the action totalled £239,582.01. The members' consent to settling on these terms was finally given at the club's annual general meeting on 22 April 1994.

Denys Rohan had judged the settlement as satisfactory. Granted, the BRDC had been advised that it had a strong case against Walkinshaw and its own directors, but such an action, if pursued, was clearly fraught with potential pitfalls. Apart from the obvious uncertainties relating to the time it might take, there was no confidence that any of the former directors, apart from Walkinshaw, would have the resources to meet the terms of any judgment that might be made against them.

In any event, the financial situation of the BRDC and Silverstone Circuits at that time was quite serious. The BRDC had outstanding borrowings of £2.25 million and had made an operating loss of £44,000 the previous year. In addition, Silverstone Circuits was bracing itself for significant additional expenditure on improving the circuit to secure the contract for the British Grand Prix beyond 1996, when the existing contract expired.

Yet this was by no means the end of the story. The BRDC then pursued a legal claim against its solicitors for the bottom-line £3 million loss this ill-starred affair had caused the club. To start with, the solicitors conceded that they had been negligent in failing to advise the board of the need for approval from the members. But they also claimed that the basic problem had not been their incorrect advice, but the fundamentally 'flawed commercial judgement' of the directors.

In summing up during the court case, it was emphasised that there was no question of dishonesty involved, but "it is quite apparent from all the evidence that the [BRDC] directors relied strongly on the fact that Mr Walkinshaw, whose supposed Midas touch was at the heart of the plan, was one of their number and would be working for them.

"In retrospect, it is difficult to understand how they can have regarded a price of £5.3 million as appropriate, given the financial information before them, and indeed by their own knowledge of the motor trade at the time.

"It can only be explained by their relationship with Mr Walkinshaw and his dominant position on the [Silverstone Circuits] board. [The lawyer advising the BRDC] was well aware of Mr Walkinshaw's special position and the importance of avoiding such conflicts. He also knew that the BRDC members included many people with considerable experience of the motor business, whose judgement on the wisdom of the deal was likely to be of considerable value." The case was won by the BRDC, which recovered all losses together with interest and costs, and the unhappy saga of Silverstone Motor Group was brought to an end.

Nicola Foulston, meanwhile, was busy running Brands Hatch Leisure and had unquestionably inherited the steel and astuteness of her father John. The millionaire founder of the Atlantic Computers company and a keen amateur racer in his own right, John Foulston purchased Brands Hatch in 1986, just over a year before he was killed, perhaps ironically, while testing a McLaren Indycar at Silverstone. At that time the Foulston family businesses, headed by his widow Mary, made the 1999 *Times* top 500 rich list in 471st place with a value of £50 million.

By this stage Nicola Foulston had established herself as an ambitious businesswoman in her own right. In 1992, at just 24 years of age, she mustered sufficient financial firepower to purchase Brands Hatch from the trust set up by her late father. Four years later Brands Hatch Leisure plc was floated on the Stock Exchange. For the next few years it thrived through a combination of aggressive marketing, tireless promotion, and a determination to find out what the spectators – or "customers", as Foulston repeatedly referred to them – wanted from their motor sport.

Yet it was her avowed intention to take over Silverstone that at a stroke rekindled the rivalry between Britain's two leading circuits, which had existed as an undercurrent within the sport for more than 30 years.

If Silverstone and the BRDC projected a stuffed-shirt image of conservatism and with it a conservative motor racing establishment, so Brands Hatch was very much home to the sandals and singlet brigade. Each community regarded the other with a tinge of wary suspicion.

"We sell the sport better; we promote it better," asserted Foulston with a breezy confidence at the start of 1999. "That's what we are good at. I believe we can lift motor racing into the lower reaches of the majority sports league rather than where it is now, which is in the middle reaches of the minority scene."

By this stage in her business career, it was Foulston's ambition to wrest control of the British Grand Prix that had so dramatically raised her profile in the UK motor sporting community. Furthermore, the suspicion that she enjoyed the tacit approval and support of Ecclestone caused a frisson of nervousness to ripple through the BRDC ranks when his Formula One Administration group signed a deal with Brands Hatch Leisure giving it the right to stage the British Grand Prix at Silverstone – when the then-current deal with the BRDC expired – in the event of her company acquiring the Northamptonshire circuit.

Ecclestone, of course, could always be relied on to inject another unpredictable twist into these unfolding events. In line with his practised policy of keeping every option open, Bernie, at the same time as endorsing the Brands Hatch Leisure bid for Silverstone, also warned that Britain could eventually lose its round of the F1 world championship unless the Northampton-shire circuit smartened up its commercial act. "No country has a God-given right to a grand prix," he said flatly. It would be a familiar theme from the commercial rights holder over the following decade as Silverstone regularly found itself put through the F1 mincing machine.

In truth, Bernie's stance effectively helped Foulston to line up a PR goal against Silverstone, which, you might be forgiven for thinking, was wholly innocent of any misdemeanour apart from trying to cut itself a commercially advantageous deal in its protracted negotiations with Ecclestone.

Foulston was quick to take the cue, insisting that this was a matter "of deep concern. If the grand prix leaves the UK, that will have an adverse effect on the whole of British motor sport," she said. "In that situation [if the BRDC retained ownership of Silverstone and did not retain the grand prix], we would step in and secure the event. We would rebuild Brands Hatch."

In truth, this was a highly provocative stance for Foulston to adopt. In summer 1999 you would have been hard pushed to find anybody within the F1 community who regarded the threat of trying to update Brands Hatch as anything more than muscle-flexing for the benefit of the media. If Foulston was going to win this high-stakes battle, the only end-game she could seriously contemplate was gaining control of Silverstone. The notion of bringing grand prix cars back to the Kent circuit was nothing more than a negotiating ploy.

Yet while Silverstone had all the facilities on its side, Brands Hatch had the topography and the reputation for being a 'better' spectator circuit. Even though it had not hosted a world championship grand prix since Nigel Mansell's victory run at the wheel of his dominant Williams-Honda some 13 years earlier.

The formal announcement of Foulston's plans had been made in spring 1999, with the publication of a lavishly presented press release from the Brands Hatch Leisure Group. In a bold and brazen style that brooked no questioning, it announced that its subsidiary, Brands Hatch Leisure Ltd, 'has signed an exclusive contract with Formula One Administration to host the British Grand Prix at Brands Hatch from 2002'.

Foulston, in her role as chief executive of Brands Hatch Leisure, was quoted as saying, 'I am delighted to have secured the future of Grand Prix racing in Britain beyond 2001. I look forward to making this the biggest and most successful Grand Prix ever, which I believe will contribute to our strategy of positioning motor sport as a truly majority sport.'

The whole tone of the press communiqué was pitched in such a way as to cause the maximum embarrassment and discomfort, making the point that 'the owner of Silverstone, the British Racing Drivers' Club, has not obtained a renewal beyond that date [2001]' and that Brands Hatch Leisure's exclusive contract had a fixed term of six years starting in 2002 with an option to renew for a further five years with the mutual agreement of Formula One Administration.

Bernie Ecclestone added, "I offered the BRDC the opportunity to renew their contract, but they felt they were not in a position to do so. I am therefore happy that I now have agreements to maintain a round of the FIA Formula One World Championship in the UK until 2007."

Brands Hatch Leisure could hardly contain its excitement, using the opportunity to announce additional plans for a £20 million package of revisions to the circuit at Brands Hatch, including the new pit and paddock complex that would be required to support a round of the F1 championship contest.

It also proudly announced that it had received 'credit committee approval' of increased funding facilities of £30 million from its bankers, Bank of Scotland, to fund the group's expansion. Craig Wilson, the bank's senior director of structured finance, noted, "BHL has undergone a significant period of expansion and development since we became the

Group's bankers in 1995. We have been happy to support BHL during this dynamic phase and look forward to being involved in the business which promises an exciting future."

It was still difficult to believe they could squeeze a state-of-the-art modern grand prix circuit into what had already seemed an extremely confined space when the British Grand Prix was last held there in 1986. But there was not even the vaguest sign of even the mildest dab of the brakes as Brands Hatch Leisure's frenzied excitement continued unchecked.

Fans were reassured that a formal detailed planning application would be submitted for consideration by the local authority. It was also pointed out that the planning application, 'in the context of Green Belt Policy', showed that the proposed scheme fell completely within a recognised area for development as set out in the Sevenoaks District Council's local plan.

A spokesman for Sevenoaks District Council added, "Brands Hatch is an important and long-established part of our district and one of the country's major sporting and leisure arenas. We recognise the venue as an asset to the area and the importance of Brands Hatch as a major local employer. We welcome the prospect of the British Grand Prix returning to Brands Hatch and look forward to working closely with the management of the company to ensure the success of the event."

By the end of March 1999, while not exactly yet on its back foot, the BRDC was certainly on the defensive as it tried accurately to read the road ahead. There was the unspoken suspicion that Foulston and Brands Hatch had somehow wormed their way on to pole position as far as Bernie Ecclestone's personal preferences were concerned. Bernie, ever the hard-nosed businessman, shrugged aside such suggestions of partiality. Yet no matter how much logic told F1 insiders that was the case, ridding oneself of the notion that Silverstone was somehow being set up for a fall was not always an easy task.

On the basis that the best form of defence can very often be attack, the BRDC made what amounted to a pre-emptive strike. On 31 March, letters from the board of directors thudded on to the doormats of the 834 club members, spelling out in no uncertain terms why they should not succumb to any tempting offers from outsiders, some of which might appeal to mercenary qualities by suggesting that individual members might benefit to the tune of between £30,000 and £50,000. It was understandable that heads might be turned by the offer of such inducements, but, within the bigger picture, they were an unwelcome distraction for the BRDC board.

The board members had to steer a careful course. Their main proposal was to set up a new company with the intention of expanding the circuit, complete with a 120-room hotel, extra car parking, and a much-needed bypass to Silverstone village.

Road access to Silverstone had long entered the motor racing history books as a potential migraine factory, yet many of its critics seemed to have forgotten just what a nightmare it had also been getting out of Brands Hatch after the 1986 British Grand Prix. When I left the press room just before midnight on the Sunday evening after that race, the Kentish lanes all around the Kent circuit were still painfully logjammed. I did not get home to Essex until just before 4am.

The underlying idea was for the new company in effect to be controlled by a 'golden share' held by the BRDC, which would provide extra room for manoeuvre when it came to vetoing future takeover bids. This whole complicated issue left the BRDC membership seething in the run-up to the club's annual general meeting, which was due to take place just over three weeks later on 23 April.

Lord Hesketh, BRDC president, said the plans, formulated with Dresdner Kleinwort Benson, were designed to "protect the club, protect Silverstone, and enfranchise the members".

Under the restructuring, the core assets of the BRDC, chiefly the Silverstone race track, would be ring-fenced and a board of guardians appointed to oversee them. The club would retain the track's freehold and rent it to a new company, Silverstone Circuits Group, which would commercialise the club's operations.

By this time, of course, the BRDC was already fighting something of a rearguard action after Foulston had gone straight to the club's members, in effect implying that the board was dragging its feet and not really doing its best in terms of looking after their interests.

Under the heading 'The Future of British Motorsport', Foulston wrote a personally signed letter to all BRDC members in what could only be interpreted as a strategy calculated to drive a wedge between the membership and the board.

It ran, 'Dear Member. In January of this year, at the invitation of your Board's financial advisor, I submitted an important proposal concerning the future of the BRDC. This proposal was not passed on to you, nor did we receive a formal response. Accordingly, I would like the opportunity to address a similar proposal directly to you, by inviting you to one of a series of presentations I shall be making across the country during July.

'Since our original approach, your Board seemed to take its foot off the pedal adopting a wait and see approach while BHL has used the time successfully to acquire the exclusive rights to host the British Grand Prix from 2002. Your Board now repeatedly comments on the difficulties of developing Brands Hatch to host the British Grand Prix – once again adopting a wait and see approach. If you don't want to wait and see, but want to hear first hand what will happen to the Grand Prix, attend one of the presentations and I will answer any of your questions.

'Your Board and BHL have spent enough money on expensive advisors (which could have been far better invested in the sport). It's time to start talking. Both BHL and the BRDC have important roles to play in the future of British motorsport. Should our proposal be accepted, the BRDC would extend its influence as a motorsport club beyond Silverstone and your existing membership rights would not only be guaranteed, but extended to our other circuits.

'BHL's proposal includes the acquisition of the commercial activities of the BRDC, together with a leasehold interest in Silverstone (leaving the freehold with the BRDC) at a price which BHL believes to be both full and fair and which makes no deduction for the loss of the contract to stage the British Grand Prix.

'If you want to have a say in shaping the future of British motorsport and have the opportunity to give me your views on BHL's proposal, please attend a presentation at one of the venues detailed overleaf. These meetings will be held in private, with no persons being admitted other than BHL, its advisors and members of the BRDC. Please bring your current membership card with you to the meetings to confirm your membership.

'I look forward to meeting you to hear your views. Kind regards. Nicky Foulston, Chief Executive.'

Seven days later the BRDC board met to discuss Foulston's

strategy and promptly despatched a letter to the entire club membership advising them to see through what the opposition seemed to be trying to do.

BRDC president Alexander Hesketh wrote, 'Ms Foulston's letter is an attempt to circumvent your board's own actions which have been designed not only to protect the future of British motorsport, but to ensure that the BRDC continues to organise the British Grand Prix and to enjoy the commercial resources to enable it to develop British motorsport and motor racing talent.

'On 24 June 1999, your board authorised Martin Brundle [representative of the BRDC board] and Denys Rohan [the chief executive of Silverstone Circuits Limited] to take all such steps as are necessary to ensure that we continue to organise the British Grand Prix at Silverstone and beyond. Since that date they have been involved in discussion with Bernie Ecclestone and various British team owners. In particular, meetings have taken place with Ron Dennis and Frank Williams, both of whom are committed to the goals of the BRDC and have agreed to be part of a four man strategy group, with Martin Brundle and Denys Rohan, to recommend a strategy to the BRDC board for the development of the BRDC which of course includes the retention of the British Grand Prix for 2002 and beyond. A letter from Ron Dennis and Frank Williams is attached.

'Your board believes that Ms Foulston's letter, which is not a formal offer, is potentially misleading. BHL's approach is not about the future of our sport or a desire to form a partnership with our club – it's about trying to buy Silverstone on the cheap.

'I therefore urge you not to deal directly with Ms Foulston

but instead to allow your board to continue to work with British team owners with a view to properly protecting your interests and those of the Silverstone circuit.

'As more fully explained in the attached letter from Ron Dennis and Frank Williams, your board believes that Brands Hatch Leisure will not be able to bring Brands Hatch up to the level required to enable it to host a Grand Prix in 2002. Accordingly time is not on BHL's side. The best interests of the BRDC will be served by taking the time to ensure that we can have a full dialogue with Bernie Ecclestone concerning the basis on which the British Grand Prix will be held in 2002 and beyond.

'Leading British teams are lining up behind your efforts. Accordingly, I should be grateful if you would confirm that you support this course of action more fully outlined in the attached letter by returning the attached form to Martin Brundle. Yours Sincerely. Alexander Hesketh, president.'

Foulston's appeal directly to the BRDC's membership rather than through the club's board of directors was not a strategy that appealed to the bosses of the UK's two leading grand prix teams, so Ron Dennis, chairman of McLaren, and Sir Frank Williams wrote an open letter to the members on 16 July 1999 urging them to disregard Nicola Foulston's approach.

In a nutshell, Dennis and Williams cast doubt over whether Brands Hatch Leisure would gain the necessary planning permission to update Brands Hatch to the requisite F1 standards and said that 'Ms Foulston's attempt to persuade the BRDC to sell her the right to stage the Grand Prix at Silverstone seems to bear out that belief.' The two team owners also pledged unequivocally to devote both their personal time 'and the resources of our various professional advisors to this task without any cost to the BRDC because we believe that the BRDC can play a leading role in the future of British motorsport'. The battle lines were clearly now being drawn.

'The barbarians are not yet exactly at the gate, but they are threatening to invade the park.' In that magisterial tone, Lord Hesketh continually urged the club's membership, seeking to apply the brakes to the enthusiasm of those who believed it would be a good idea to cut a deal with Nicola Foulston and the Brands Hatch brigade.

'At Silverstone we have a successful, expanding and well managed business turning over more than £30m,' wrote Hesketh. 'Indeed, this very success is attracting predators. At the core of BHL's proposal is the requirement for us to grant them a 50 year lease over all our freehold properties and facilities in return for £43m. What is not evident is that for a period of 50 years the club is, I believe, likely to be inadequately funded, receiving only a peppercorn rent under the lease, with no rent reviews.'

Hesketh also claimed that there were 'other aspects' to the proposal that were potentially misleading, including the claim that Brands Hatch Leisure had invested £24 million since 1996 in its circuits. He wrote, 'Scrutiny of their accounts will show some £16m spent to acquire their own freeholds and only some £8m on improvements. By comparison we have spent more than £22m on improvements at Silverstone alone over five years and believe our circuit and facilities to be second to none.'

Hesketh rounded off his letter to the members with this assessment of the situation: 'Finally, let me stress once again that BHL is a public company whose first responsibility is to its shareholders. The BRDC reinvests its profits in the infrastructure of Silverstone for the promotion of motorsport, young drivers, suitable charitable causes and for the members' benefit.

'If the membership sell out to Nicola Foulston our primary objectives will be unattainable and BHL could be sold to another public company at any time. What then for the future of Silverstone and British motor sport?'

Yet Foulston was not prepared to blink at the height of this confrontation and raised the ante even further by suggesting that, if the BRDC was not willing to cut a deal with her, she would consider running the UK's round of the F1 world championship outside the country, possibly even in Africa. This story grabbed the sports pages of Britain's national daily newspapers by the throat. In essence, Foulston said she was prepared to spell the end of 76 years of British motor racing history if the local planners did not give Brands Hatch Leisure the necessary permission to upgrade the Brands Hatch circuit to the standards required to run the British Grand Prix.

Foulston told the *Daily Mail*, "I'm not saying to the planners, 'Give me permission or I'll take the British Grand Prix overseas', because that is implicitly understood. We are planning to develop new race tracks in Asia, Latin America and Africa, where we could hold it. Two developments should be announced this year."

She also insisted that she had the full support of Bernie Ecclestone when it came to making such assertions, claiming that there were precedents, in that the San Marino Grand Prix took place at Imola in Italy and the 1982 Swiss Grand Prix was staged at Dijon-Prenois in France.

FIA spokesman Francesco Longanesi confirmed to the *Daily Mail*, "Technically what Nicola Foulston says is right. We have the examples of San Marino and Switzerland, although the difference is that there are no circuits in San Marino and motor racing is banned in Switzerland.

"Theoretically, it could be done, although it would need the approval of the RAC, which runs the sport in Britain, and the FIA. If she decided to stage the grand prix in another country without permission, it would be an unofficial race and would not count towards the world championship. But one possibility, although an unlikely one, could be that there was no British Grand Prix at all."

By November 1999 the BRDC was marshalling its forces in a bid to hang on to the grand prix.

Alexander Hesketh had tentatively discussed the possibility of an amalgamation between the Silverstone and Brands Hatch businesses, but Foulston was having none of it. Now she had the signatures that mattered on a contract for the British Grand Prix. It was coming down to a bare-knuckle fight between Foulston and the BRDC.

But there was some distance to go before the matter was totally resolved. Any notion that Hesketh might somehow be able to broker a deal whereby the BRDC and Brands Hatch could get together to offer a united negotiating stance with Ecclestone was of no interest to this driven and highly motivated young lady.

What subsequently emerged, however, is that Foulston had been talking privately with Les Delano, who was a director of Octagon Motorsport. This was the sports marketing and entertainment division of the New York-based Interpublic Group, one of the world's largest advertising and marketing communications groups. This was a clever strategy, for Foulston, who was aiming to maximise her personal wealth by ramping up the value of her investment in Brands Hatch by – ultimately – selling to the highest bidder, was talking on two separate fronts. On the one hand she was talking to the BRDC to keep open her commitment to Ecclestone to run the British Grand Prix, while at the same time she was manoeuvring herself into a position where she might be able to sell her entire business empire for a massive profit.

By the middle of 1999 Foulston was ready with her ultimate plan to extricate herself personally from the motor racing business. She formally advised Ecclestone that she was selling Brands Hatch to Octagon, explaining away this decision on the basis that she needed to raise extra funds to update the Kent circuit in time to be ready to run the 2002 British Grand Prix there, as she was required to do under the terms of her contract with him.

Yet Nicola Foulston would be long out of the equation before the 2000 F1 season began.

Brands Hatch duly fell into American hands when its owner accepted a £120 million takeover bid from the Interpublic Group.

At the end of the day, the board of Brands Hatch Leisure voted unanimously to accept the offer of 22.67 new Interpublic shares for every Brands Hatch share, valuing each share at approximately 546p.

Nicola, whose family trust was the largest shareholder in Brands Hatch, had given undertakings to accept the deal unless a third party offered more in cash.

Analysts believed at the time that that was unlikely, with Interpublic's offer already pitched at a heady 37.4 times the previous year's earnings. Assuming the remaining investors voted to accept, Brands Hatch would become part of Octagon.

Octagon already operated the popular superbike world championship at Brands Hatch. Foulston, whose trust stood to receive around £35 million-worth of Interpublic shares for its 29.8 per cent holding, was confirmed as joining the board of Octagon and would continue to oversee the development of the Brands Hatch site.

Brands Hatch owned three other circuits: Oulton Park, Snetterton, and Cadwell Park. Its shares climbed 21.5p to 515p after the deal was announced, but still closed 31p short of the 546p offer price. Institutional shareholders that voted to accept the bid were expected to sell their Interpublic shares as soon as possible.

Foulston insisted the deal was right for shareholders. "Our vision has long been to be the leading international event promoter and venue manager in world motor sports," she said. "To achieve this we need to expand our operations from our UK base around the world."

Brands Hatch already had one overseas race track in its sights. But Foulston was unlikely to renew the abortive bid for Silverstone, home of the British Grand Prix.

Dealing with Ecclestone was always an instructive process and the BRDC would come to learn over the years that followed that the process was something akin to defusing an unexploded bomb, in the sense that, if one tried to get pushy or aggressive, the whole process could blow up in your face.

Yet at the end of the day Foulston walked away from what had been the family business barely a month after the sale to Octagon had been finalised. Citing 'personal reasons', she was succeeded by Rob Bain as the new Brands Hatch Leisure chief executive; he had originally joined the company in 1998 as financial director. Foulston's contract allowed her to leave in the event of a change in ownership of the business. It was also reported at the time that her managing director Richard Green had a similar proviso in his contract and he departed the company with considerable benefits.

Life would never prove to be easy for Silverstone in the early years of the new millennium, with seemingly one niggling problem following after another. Nicola Foulston may now have been history as far as the negotiations for the future of the British Grand Prix were concerned, but there were still deep anxieties over precisely what was going to happen as far as the British Grand Prix beyond 2001 was concerned.

Ken Tyrrell, the former world championship-winning F1 team owner, had by the start of 2000 taken over as club president from Alexander Hesketh. Having sold his Tyrrell F1 team to British American Tobacco for around $13 million back in 1998, he had agreed to take on the role at the BRDC through a sense of obligation to both the club and the sport. But even when he agreed to take up the position, Ken knew that it could not be an open-ended commitment because he was already suffering with the cancer that would carry him to his grave by the late summer of 2001.

Yet Tyrrell did a good job rallying the troops, peppering his communications with dry humour and irony. 'As a number of members have pointed out,' he noted in a letter to the members in April 2000, 'if it wasn't for the commercial success of the club over the past decade nobody would have been interested in us anyway, so in that respect we have become victims of our own success!'

He added, 'Nor can Silverstone stand apart from the rapidly changing world. Nonetheless, with the uncertainties behind us, the commercial management's time will once again be dedicated wholeheartedly to continuing to grow the Club's commercial status and success, without distraction, leaving the BRDC board to concentrate on club matters and its supervisory role.'

Yet none of these words provided the soothing balm some BRDC members were so keenly looking for. One lobbying group was informally headed by Sir John Whitmore, who had been a successful sports and touring car driver in the 1960s. He and his supporters clearly felt that the BRDC board was being excessively defensive in its dealings with Brands Hatch and had not correctly assessed the potential benefits of such an alliance.

'A similar situation arose a few years ago over the Tom Walkinshaw affair,' he recalled in an open letter dated 8 August 1999. 'Unbusinesslike actions by the BRDC board were followed by emotive reactions from, shall we say, the more competitive members. What does this tell us? BRDC members and the management team they elect are not the best people to manage what has become – and not entirely due to their skill – a very large and multi-faceted business. Unfortunately they do not seem to be able to select the best professional advisors either. The most expensive perhaps...'

Whitmore continued, 'I suspect that Ecclestone's contract with BHL is pretty watertight and that the only way of ensuring that the Grand Prix remains at Silverstone is actually to negotiate sensibly with BHL for just that.

'If the BRDC do not do this, the Grand Prix will move to Brands Hatch provided planning permission is assured, and I believe it will be because I live in Kent and I know that the council is sympathetic. Silverstone will lose the British Grand Prix and therefore much of its income and its value. Is that good stewardship of the assets of the club when the opportunity of a joint venture of some sort would enable the Grand Prix to stay at Silverstone?'

In the event, Whitmore was to be proved incorrect in his prediction that Brands Hatch would get planning permission to update its circuit. However, in spring 2000 the BRDC had to face yet another problem on yet another front, as a consequence of the FIA's decision to allocate the British Grand Prix the unseasonably early date of 23 April rather than its regular summer slot on the international calendar.

For the fans, the result of the race itself was a matter for celebration, even though behind the scenes there was tension and unpleasantness. David Coulthard took a leaf out of Nigel Mansell's book with a memorably bold overtaking manoeuvre to clinch his second straight victory in the British Grand Prix, a record previously achieved by Mansell with his Williams-Renault in 1991 and 1992.

Coulthard took the chequered flag just 1.4 seconds ahead of his McLaren-Mercedes team-mate Mika Häkkinen after a flawless performance that vaulted him into second place in the drivers' championship behind Ferrari's Michael Schumacher, who finished third.

The golden moment for the 29-year-old Scot came on lap 31 of the hotly contested fourth round of the title chase, when he was shadowing the leading Ferrari F1 2000 of Rubens Barrichello, who had started from pole position.

Barrichello suffered a slight gear-change glitch going through the daunting 140mph Becketts S-bend and Coulthard got a run at him coming out on to the 190mph Hangar Straight. It was a move that reprised Mansell's epic victory over his Williams-Honda team-mate Nelson Piquet here 13 years before, as DC forced his way around the outside of the Ferrari to take the lead.

It was an upbeat end to a weekend on which Silverstone had been virtually flooded and the public car parks had had to be closed for Saturday qualifying in a vain effort to improve things for race day. Yet such a step could not forestall the inevitable outpourings of acrimony that swirled around the circuit owners, organisers, and the FIA. The governing body in particular came under much fire for sanctioning the unseasonably early Easter date for the British race rather than its regular July place on the calendar.

Things had got even worse on race day. The combination of a capacity crowd and slow progress in gaining access to the spectator car parks caused a total seizure to the traffic flow around the circuit. Despite warnings from the police not even to try joining the 15-mile traffic jams to gain entry to the circuit, a 60,000-strong crowd displayed remarkable grit and determination to gain access to a venue that looked more like the Glastonbury rock festival than a high-profile international sporting venue.

There was also an unfortunate PR own-goal on the part of the BRDC, in that the 2000 British Grand Prix marked the opening of a new £2 million clubhouse overlooking Woodcote corner. This inevitably, if unfortunately, gave the club's critics more ammunition to browbeat the owners of Silverstone. With spectators suffering in sodden silence beneath the unwelcome downpour, all they could see was the BRDC glitterati swanning around in sumptuous comfort within their new gilded cage.

It was only a short mental jump from that point to suggesting that it was a wanton waste of cash that the club should look after its own in such luxury when the expenditure ought to have been focused on making life more enjoyable for the folk who had spent their hard-earned cash to come through the turnstiles into the public enclosure.

It was unfortunate that the truth of the matter could not have been more widely circulated, in that none of the money for constructing the clubhouse had come from spectator income streams. It had been funded in its totality by the one-off payment of damages from the legal action against the club's then solicitors who had given incorrect advice to the BRDC on the matter of the Walkinshaw/Silverstone Motor Group controversy several years earlier. But that message was never communicated properly by the club to the outside world, with the result that the sniggering about the BRDC's perceived elitist and out-of-touch demeanour would linger on for many years whenever the question of the clubhouse was raised.

While some insiders minced their words, triple world champion Jackie Stewart, who later in the year would take over as BRDC president from Ken Tyrrell, held the sport's governing body to blame for the fiasco that resulted in the paying public being turned away from Saturday's qualifying session for the British race.

Describing the sequence of events that led up to the rescheduling of the race as "scandalous", he said that the whole episode was a major disaster for the sport as a whole.

"It is terrible for F1," said Stewart firmly. "It's terrible for the corporate partners of the teams, terrible for the fans, and bad for all our industry. But this is not Silverstone's fault. The governing body chooses the dates, not Silverstone. All major professional sporting events follow the sun. I don't care whether you are talking about the Masters, the Kentucky Derby, Ascot, or the British Grand Prix. Would they put the Italian Grand Prix on in April? Of course they would not. Why? Because it would probably be pouring with rain as it was here."

Even as Stewart delivered his carefully judged critique, a forlorn, windswept poster on the exit road to Silverstone touted a July date for the 2001 British Grand Prix 'subject to confirmation' – an ironic twist on a weekend when torrential rain forced the race organisers to turn away Saturday's spectators due to the glutinous state of the near-flooded car parks.

Amid this shock, dismay, and disbelief within the motor racing community, there had been a lighter moment during Friday's free practice session that somehow seemed to put the whole awful dilemma into an ironic perspective.

F1 powerbroker Ecclestone had been striding down the paddock, not really watching where he was going as he chatted to one of his acolytes, when he stepped in the only deep puddle within 20 metres. Apart from the fact that puddles are not generally permitted access to the exclusive environs of the F1 paddock – and the fact that we are not privileged to know just how much Mr Ecclestone pays for his footwear – this seemed, in some people's minds, an appropriate reward for the multi-billionaire who many felt should shoulder the blame for the whole sorry fiasco.

On the other hand, it might have seemed a harsh judgement on Ecclestone, for had Silverstone been blessed by fine Easter weather its move from its traditional summer date would not have mattered in the slightest. But even giving Bernie the benefit of the doubt, the fact is that moving the British Grand Prix from its original summer date amounted to a major disruption to the British sporting eco-system. Like Royal Ascot, Henley, and Wimbledon, Britain's round of the world championship is associated with sunny afternoons and long evenings. Not cold, miserable rain.

"It's not my fault," said Bernie firmly. "Don't blame me. Internal [motor racing] politics caused the change of date. It is disappointing for the spectators, but not something that Silverstone could have done anything about. Someone had to have this date in the calendar and Silverstone agreed to it. But it didn't work. Don't blame them for not knowing that the weather was going to be like this."

However, Ken Tyrrell made it clear that he felt Bernie knew exactly what the implications of such a date change would be. "What we're seeing here must surely tell everyone – even Bernie – that the time for the British Grand Prix is certainly not in April," he said. "And I think even Bernie recognises that if the race was held at Brands Hatch or Donington Park at the same time, it would be raining there as well."

McLaren's team principal Ron Dennis took a more conciliatory tone, insisting that although it was not Silverstone's fault, the scheduling of the event on this early date was "not malicious". He added, "It has rained pretty well consistently for 15 days, which was always going to give any promoter a major problem. But it has to be said that whoever has the challenge of putting the international calendar together has a juggling job to do."

It was perhaps inevitable that some cynics reflected on the reaction of the organisers of the 1993 European Grand Prix at Donington as an example of what Silverstone should have done. Faced with similarly torrential rain in the run-up to that Easter Sunday event, Tom Wheatcroft had started a crash programme to asphalt all his public car parks only days before the race.

Even so, he lost a reputed £3 million on that race and F1 had not been back to Donington since. The point, of course, is that most of the races on the European calendar would have faced the same dilemma with sodden car parks had their fixtures taken place in such inhospitable conditions.

This was by no means the end of Silverstone's problems, however. Barely two months after the washout, it became clear that the FIA was effectively holding the circuit responsible for the Easter fiasco. The FIA World Motor Sport Council, meeting in Warsaw a few days after the 2000 Canadian GP, made it clear that the 2001 race was under threat unless the circuit could address and rectify the supposed organisational problems that had blighted the race.

Definite inclusion on the calendar, Silverstone was warned, would depend on confirmation from FIA safety delegate Charlie Whiting that changes to procedures in Silverstone race control had been implemented and on satisfactory plans showing how the circuit and police would ensure that there would be no repetition of the traffic problems that arose in 2000.

Furthermore, as if to add insult to injury, the FIA demanded a report detailing how ticket-holding spectators who had been unable to enter the circuit on Saturday would be compensated by Silverstone.

However, the Motor Sports Association and the BRDC felt confident that they could meet these exacting standards – even though you might be forgiven for wondering if it was worth bothering, given that the race was still theoretically moving to Brands Hatch for 2002, which Octagon was still dreaming about, even though anybody who knew anything about anything in the F1 business knew there would not be a snowflake's chance in hell of that happening.

In retrospect, the Motor Sports Association and the BRDC adopted an uncomfortably supine and deferential position towards the governing body. Depressing, naturally, but they had little choice. Faced with the FIA seemingly wanting to drain every drop of blood from their veins, there was no option but to smile sweetly and defer with as much dignity as they could muster.

At least Jackie Stewart called a spade a spade, as usual. "I am very disappointed that the July date has not been restored," he said, "because it has been traditional for a number of years. Since Britain is the capital of motor sport it seems to me wrong that our race has not been given a time more suitable.

"However, I am sure that the MSA and the BRDC will ensure that all of the appropriate conditions to run the race will be provided, as they have been all these years until the extreme conditions which prevailed at this year's race which was held on a date demanded by the FIA."

Jackie was duly elected BRDC president in 2000, shortly after the British Grand Prix had taken place. By this time, the club was in the throes of detailed discussions with Interpublic to ensure that the contract Interpublic had originally inherited from Nicola Foulston would enable it to run the race at Silverstone from 2002, given that it was clear that Brands Hatch was by now a non-starter. Even if planning permission had been granted, the reality was that there just wasn't enough room at Brands Hatch to construct a circuit to the necessary standard.

As a result, a deal was agreed whereby Interpublic would lease Silverstone from the BRDC for £8 million a year, with the BRDC retaining all its members' rights. In Jackie Stewart's words, "this was an amazingly good financial arrangement for the BRDC – perhaps too good – and it seemed to secure the future of the race".

Unfortunately a complaint was subsequently lodged with the UK's Competition Commission, alleging that the BRDC's deal with Interpublic gave it control of more than 20 per cent of the racing circuits in the UK. The issue dragged on for many months, taking up huge amounts of time for both Stewart and Martin Brundle, who had been appointed BRDC chairman.

The two of them were run ragged by the events of the four years they served on the board. That time can best be summed up by Brundle's advice to me when he heard that I was standing for election to the BRDC board in 2004: "I've got only three words to say to you," he warned. "Don't do it." I nodded sagely in agreement and then proceeded to ignore Martin's wise counsel. After two nerve-racking years on the board I concluded that he had been right and I had been wrong.

Jackie Stewart put his similar feelings into pin-sharp perspective in his autobiography *Winning is Not Enough* when he said, 'What followed was a difficult period of my life when I worked hard to safeguard the future of the circuit [Silverstone] and the British Grand Prix but felt increasingly isolated among the demanding F1 authorities, apathetic politicians and a club in which there was a vocal body resistant to change.'

He added, 'There were many times when I felt like walking

away from all the hassle, from the internal politics and different agendas, but I stuck it out because I had made my promise to Ken and also because I felt an obligation to "do my bit" for British motorsport. It may sound trite, but the reality was that I felt that the sport had been good to me and I wanted to give something back.'

To be fair, it was only a small minority of individuals who proved to be vociferous troublemakers. They, it can be argued, contributed little to the BRDC, in contrast to the main body of the membership, most of whom were positive and totally committed to doing the best for the club.

Getting through the 2001 British Grand Prix with no more problems was the immediate priority for the BRDC and, although the race was now back in its traditional July date, there was certainly an underlying nervousness that any fresh problems could jeopardise the event's very future.

Transport to and from the event had never been straight-forward but over the past two years the problem had grown into a crisis and memories of that Easter fiasco loomed large in everyone's memories.

A repeat this weekend could end the race that started modern motor racing when it first ran in 1950, but thanks to a major programme of renovation organisers were confident that problems on such a scale would be avoided.

"We've spent £17 million this year putting in extra car parking and perimeter roads around the circuit, and we're going to spend a further £23 million by May next year," said Rob Bain, chief executive of Octagon Motorsports, which was running the first British Grand Prix of its supposed 15-year contract.

"The new set-up will completely change the traffic. Obviously when you're moving 20,000 vehicles in the space of an hour there are going to be traffic problems anywhere in the world, but the traffic flows will be markedly improved compared to previous years."

They would need to be. The previous December Octagon had been forced to lodge a $5 million bond with the FIA to underline the seriousness with which it was approaching the problem. The money was returned two weeks before the 2001 race, after the completion of the circuit's new access road. But the A43, which would carry fans to the circuit from the M1 and M40, was not yet finished and would be only partially opened for the first time on race weekend.

"It's a bit disappointing that the A43 isn't finished, but that's primarily because when the work started it was immediately stopped again because of foot and mouth and the contractors have never quite managed to catch up," said Rob Tinlin, chief executive of South Northamptonshire Council.

In fact Jackie Stewart had managed to raise £8m from the government for this first section of the new approach roads to be at least half completed for 2001, meeting with two Cabinet ministers at the Highways Agency at the instigation of the then prime minister Tony Blair.

"We've spent the last six months working to make sure the traffic management is as good as we can get it for this year," said Tinlin. "So I'm quite confident that it should run smoothly, barring accidents. But there's still a lot of work to do and the threat of losing the grand prix from Britain hasn't gone away."

In an effort to minimise traffic congestion, Octagon cut capacity for the 2001 event by a third, to 60,000. But its confidence in the new arrangements was such that it had already decided to increase capacity to the original 90,000 for 2002. Tickets, held until the end of September at 2001 prices, were already available for the 2002 race.

By summer 2002 the second phase of Octagon's improvements – upgrading the pit and paddock, the hospitality suites, and the media centre – was due to be complete. "When it's finished, it will be spot on," said Tinlin. "From this autumn you'll be able to drive from the motorway straight up a dual carriageway and into the car park."

Local police were quietly confident of a less problematic day at the races in 2001 than anyone had experienced of late. "People should be prepared for slight delays but we're hopeful that traffic will be moving in and out of Silverstone pretty smoothly," said a spokesman.

Bain added: "I hope there will be no repeat of the warnings we've had from the FIA in the past. Hopefully they'll see the commitment we've made to resolve the issues they've had in the past."

Unfortunately Rob Bain's experiences at Silverstone in 2002 were not so pleasant. He had one particularly disgruntled customer and that was the most important customer of all, Bernie Ecclestone. The helicopter carrying the F1 commercial rights holder had to be diverted at the last moment and the driver of the car sent to collect him briefly got lost, a slip which Bernie attributed to the poor signposting within the circuit.

Ecclestone criticised the lack of adequate signposting, saying that the event felt like a "country fair masquerading as a world event". Bain stood his ground and argued that Bernie was being unfair, claiming that feedback from customers suggested that this was not the case. That might well have been so, but Bain missed a golden opportunity to keep his mouth firmly shut. It was neither the time nor the place to cross swords so publicly with Bernie Ecclestone. The following day Bain resigned.

Octagon also faced problems relating to the issue of upgrading the circuit facilities in line with the exacting requirements laid out by Ecclestone and endorsed by FIA president Max Mosley. In response to this pressure Silverstone committed to a so-called 'master plan' to transform the circuit into a facility that would be the envy of the international motor sport community. This would not only include the long-awaited new pits, paddock, and grandstands, but also an interactive visitors' centre, a hotel, and a restaurant. The massive cost would be in the order of £80 million, with half being split between Ecclestone, the BRDC, and Octagon, buttressed by the hope that the government could be persuaded to contribute the balance.

Yet Bernie prevaricated, sat on the paperwork, and never got around to signing off the plan. It was a worrying time. As long as the most powerful man in motor racing withheld his formal approval, then the circuit upgrade could not go ahead. That in turn meant that the FIA might drop Silverstone from the F1 world championship schedule. Following logically on from that was the possibility of Silverstone losing much of its value and Octagon being left saddled with a 15-year promoter's deal with Ecclestone and no circuit on which to hold the race.

By autumn 2002 it was clear that Octagon was in a state of near panic. Having been lured into the motor racing business by the convincing and plausible sales pitch delivered to it by Nicola Foulston, the group began to realise that the F1 business was a bottomless black hole into which it was being required to shovel money at an alarmingly prodigious and profligate rate.

Octagon's parent Interpublic had watched its stock price in New York tumbling as Octagon's losses ballooned, wiping out over 30 per cent of the group's quoted share value. By March 2003 it had decided that it wanted out of its motor racing commitments but, with binding commitments to pay the BRDC for operating Silverstone and to Ecclestone's companies for the long-term race fees, it was difficult to see who would be interested in buying.

Jonathan Palmer's MotorSport Vision organisation eventually bought all Octagon's circuits except Silverstone for a knock-down price. But getting out of the commitment to Ecclestone and to the BRDC was to prove an even more numbing experience.

In April 2004, Interpublic agreed to pay Ecclestone's companies a total of $93 million over five years, while the BRDC would be left to negotiate its own separate settlement with the American corporation as regards its obligation towards Silverstone.

This was a most disagreeable and bad-tempered period for the owners of Silverstone. In spring 2004 I was elected to the BRDC's board. Ray Bellm had been appointed chairman in succession to Martin Brundle. Bellm, whose family had made a fortune from pharmaceuticals, was an accomplished driver, having won the C2 sports car world championship on three occasions. The way Bellm saw it was that he had been elected to the job because of his entrepreneurial ability and the fact that he was prepared to stand up to Jackie Stewart who, some members felt, was exerting too much influence and authority in his role as the club's president.

Bellm, while cordial and pleasant enough company, clearly

had little respect for most other members of the board, me included, who he quickly decided were lightweights when it came to business dealings at this sort of level. To be honest, he was correct in that assessment, but that wasn't really the point. One of the BRDC's attractive qualities – that it is a very broad church indeed – is also its most frustrating feature. Some of us were struggling to keep up, but Bellm also seemed to think that we lacked minds of our own and simply did what Jackie Stewart told us. On the other hand, Bellm always struck me as the sort of guy who would be prone to losing his hair-trigger temper if he did not get his way. As I said, the membership was a 'broad church'.

Interpublic duly approached Silverstone to sort out the cost of an exit strategy before it was bled dry. Bellm flew to New York with BRDC chief executive Alex Hooton and a mandate from the board to agree a settlement within the terms of reference previously agreed by the board. At the end of the day Interpublic agreed to pay £27 million in staged payments, which in effect reflected its obligations until the end of 2007.

As Terry Lovell wrote, 'The deal ... finally brought to a close a monumental fiasco that cost IPG an estimated £500m.' But in retrospect, that was the easy bit, for the BRDC at least. There was still the issue of negotiating an extension to the BRDC's contract with Ecclestone from 2005 onwards. These discussions were painfully protracted by any standards.

The BRDC opened the bidding by proposing a three-year deal covering the 2005 to 2007 races starting at $10.8 million in 2005 and escalating at the rate of inflation for the balance of the contract. Bernie responded by saying he wanted $15.9 million for 2005 and then $17.3 million for 2006, which he claimed were fees in line with other European races. Then he offered a seven-year deal starting at $13.5 million and escalating at 10 per cent annually – which would have had the effect of more than doubling the fee over the seven-year period – or a five-year deal from 2007 with no races in 2005 and 2006.

The big-budget tennis game continued into the autumn. Ecclestone then offered two further revised proposals. One was a seven-year deal at $13.5 million a year but with an obligation that the BRDC should build the new pits and paddock facilities that had been discussed at length for a couple of years. The other was for Ecclestone to take over as promoter of the race, with his companies taking rent-free possession for that period and the club funding the new pit infrastructure but not taking any income from the race. Neither proposal was judged acceptable by the club.

Ecclestone came back with his final offer: an initial one-year deal with an option for a further six with a starting fee of $13.5 million escalating at 10 per cent per annum. The BRDC responded with two more counter-proposals but it seemed as though Bernie had run out of patience.

There was another interesting dimension to the whole question of the BRDC cutting a deal with Ecclestone to extend the contract for the race beyond 2005.

Jackie Stewart supported a three-year deal because that, in his view, would give Silverstone more negotiating flexibility in the longer term. This, he felt, would be beneficial because there was a fear that the major F1 motor manufacturers involved in the sport might carry out their threat and start an independent series once the present Concorde Agreement – the detailed protocol that bound the teams to compete in the official FIA world championship – expired at the end of 2007.

Certainly, from the BRDC board's vantage point in 2004, this was a possibility, even though with the benefit of hindsight it was going to take a huge leap of faith on the part of the car makers to take such an initiative. In any event, Ecclestone knew that Ferrari would be the key to the future success of any world championship, official or otherwise, and he took care to ensure that the famous Maranello team was offered preferential financial terms that would keep it firmly on-side in the longer term. Also, it was hard to foresee the economic depression that would eventually send Honda, BMW, and Toyota scrambling for the F1 exit door in 2009 and 2010.

Whether Ecclestone should even have been asking Silverstone for more cash was also a bone of contention. Jackie Stewart felt that it was wholly unreasonable for him to ask for payment to renew the race contract from 2005, given that he had effectively been paid for these races through the terms of the Interpublic severance settlement. Bernie, not unexpectedly, did not see it this way and claimed that what he had offered the BRDC was "totally fair".

Even Bellm would have to agree that although gaining a consensus among the BRDC board members was a tricky balancing act, it was a piece of cake compared with reconciling the interests and ambitions of the 800-odd members of the club proper. The qualities that gel to produce a competitive racing driver – self-absorbed determination and the belief that you can do the job better than the next man – can be simply tiresome and slightly baffling when seeking a compromise agreement across a wide variety of issues.

Of course, on the opposite side of the equation was Ecclestone, running his one-man ship with matchless mental dexterity, controlling every negotiating move and controlling every shot. He had a mandate from both the teams and his colleagues at CVC Capital Partners, to whom he had sold his share of the F1 commercial rights in 2005, to do the best job he could. And he did that unrelentingly.

There was another crucial dimension that affected the stance of the BRDC board to negotiating an extension of the British Grand Prix contract beyond 2005. This was detailed debate over just how long the new contract should be for, an issue that was almost more important than the money itself.

The matter came to a head when Bellm incurred the wrath of Sir Jackie by effectively trying to deliver a fait accompli by arriving at a meeting with the BRDC lawyers and accountants to announce that he had signed a five-year deal with Ecclestone the previous evening. Stewart was furious, criticising Bellm for exceeding his authority by not referring the proposed length of the contract back to the BRDC board for ratification before he appended his signature.

Bellm brushed aside these concerns and insisted that he had not exceeded his mandate. It was now crunch time between Bellm and Sir Jackie. On 11 January 2005 Bellm was voted off the board by six votes to three and resigned as chairman. He accused those of us who voted against him of being led by the nose by Sir Jackie. The way I remember it is that if we had backed Bellm we would have lost Stewart immediately. To a degree, we were voting for the 'least bad' outcome, given that one of them was going to go.

Bellm's successor as chairman was the highly regarded Stuart Rolt, whose father Tony was one of the sport's oldest and most respected grandees, having shared the winning Jaguar C-type with Duncan Hamilton in the 1953 Le Mans 24-hour classic.

There was more to come. It was quite clear that with the £27 million paid by Interpublic to the BRDC, there was sufficient money in the club's kitty to give it some much-needed breathing space when it came to paying the race sanctioning fee to Ecclestone's Formula One Management Group. Or it could have been used to upgrade Silverstone. But there was not enough to do both. The board's solution to this was to open negotiations with various property developers who might be interested in a mutually advantageous joint venture to share the risk of upgrading the circuit to cater for the sport's long-term future.

Meanwhile, the 2005 British Grand Prix came and went in fine style with Juan Pablo Montoya scoring a memorable victory for the McLaren-Mercedes squad and in so doing beating Renault's Fernando Alonso, the world champion elect, into second place.

It was also a weekend fuelled by speculation that Jenson Button would be off to join Michael Schumacher at Ferrari in 2006 as part of a $20 million deal, but this turned out not to be the case and was denied by Button. As it happened, there would be movement in the other direction, with Schumacher's Ferrari team-mate Rubens Barrichello leaving Maranello to join Button in the BAR – soon to be Honda – squad.

Button was also presented the Mike Hawthorn Trophy by sports minister Richard Caborn in recognition of his performances for BAR during the 2004 season. This award is made annually to the most successful British or Commonwealth driver in F1.

The Silverstone race was also where the FIA and AMD

published the detailed results of a survey they had carried out with 93,000 F1 fans. According to the feedback, 94 per cent wanted more overtaking, 74 per cent wanted more emphasis on driver skill, 69 per cent wanted more teams to be competing, and 84 per cent wanted 18 or more races each season. The fans were also insistent that they wanted high technology to remain as a key element underpinning the sport's appeal.

By the start of 2006 the BRDC board was ready to confirm that its preferred partner was St Modwen Properties plc, which proposed a wide-ranging and extremely ambitious £600 million investment on a 150-year lease, under the terms of which the club would receive a £30 million advance that would enable the pressing issue of building new pits and paddock facilities to be addressed as an immediate priority.

By now, however, the BRDC membership had clearly had enough of the board's deliberations and, in a move that I always felt reflected this reality rather than the intrinsic belief that the St Modwen deal was a bad one, the proposal was shelved for good in April 2006.

Foremost among those members opposed to the St Modwens deal was Harry Stiller, the winner of the 1966 British F3 championship. He disputed the mathematics used to justify the validity of the deal with the Birmingham-based property developers. In the end the proposed collaboration was consigned to history, as was Stiller from the club's membership after his application for life membership revealed gaps during the past 40 years, which turned out to be periods detained at Her Majesty's pleasure.

Stewart indicated that he would be standing down from his role as BRDC president at the 2006 annual general meeting and endorsed Damon Hill as his successor. The 1996 world champion's late father, Graham, had been Jackie's team-mate and mentor during his first season driving in F1 for the BRM team in 1965.

But the membership had a sting in its tail for the outgoing triple champion. A group of dissenters proposed a vote of no confidence in Jackie and a vote of no confidence in the board. Both were soundly defeated, due very much to Stewart's relentless wooing of the membership over a relatively short period of time. I personally found it deeply satisfying when the voting results were announced – and Jackie's expression looked very much like that of the Lion King. It was a salutary reminder that you took on this driven man absolutely at your peril.

By March 2007 the race was on again to snap up Silverstone, home of the British Grand Prix. Property developer Oliver Speight, chairman of Spectre, had tabled an opening offer of £56 million for the 800-acre site, which the board of the BRDC was considering.

Though Damon insisted that Silverstone was not for sale, the truth was that the members could not afford to redevelop the circuit themselves to meet the international standards set by the super facilities of Malaysia, China, and Turkey.

Damon Hill acknowledged the Spectre offer and said, "We're not planning to sell Silverstone – that's not the objective. We've got a plan that we're proceeding with in order to develop the circuit.

"It's quite common for people, especially property developers, to approach anyone with a property and make a proposal. He [Speight] has written to all the members, which was not strictly correct etiquette, and made an offer to buy the asset. The BRDC board have responded to that in the correct way and it will be looked at thoroughly.

"We have a self-funded approach to the development of the circuit. We will get planning permission, it will raise the asset value of the property, and then we will borrow against that to develop the circuit. That was also okayed by the members."

CHAPTER FIVE

THE MAN YOU DEAL WITH

Bernie Ecclestone is ultimately the man you have to get on your side if you want to secure a world championship grand prix. He has high standards and is not known to make the process of compromise easy. But this is a rite of passage to be experienced by all aspiring grand prix promoters. And seasoned ones, too, as Silverstone was about to find out.

Understanding Bernie Ecclestone is the key to having a peaceful life in the upper reaches of the F1 business. The reality, of course, is that this is much more complicated than it sounds. The real key is understanding that you *don't* have a complete understanding of how his mind works. All you can be pretty certain of is that it works faster than yours does. In the context of the battle for the British Grand Prix, it is worth considering his persona and methods in more detail.

The newcomer within the F1 community must tread both carefully and discreetly. Ecclestone is an absolute stickler for minute detail and never forgets a slight. You always think twice before replying to anything he says or acting on it too hastily. He seldom misses an opportunity to offer subtly barbed observations, delivered with deadpan insouciance, which leaves the interviewer suspended in what often feels like thin air.

In an excellent article by Cole Moreton published in the *Mail on Sunday* on the morning of the 2010 Bahrain Grand Prix, the interviewer established that Ecclestone would be happy to die, when his time comes, at a grand prix. Moreton asked as a supplement, since Bernie would clearly die in luxury, what would his comments be to the race fans who sit in rickety grandstands at Silverstone's Club corner?

"I don't know," he replied crisply with a directness that would unsettle most interviewers. "I've never been up there." Then he neatly turned the tables on his inquisitor by adding, "The truth of the matter is that you, unfortunately, went to Silverstone. It's what Britain does well. Anything downmarket.

"At other races you'd find it was a hell of a lot better. Silverstone and British races have always been a bit amateur and clubby, because the people who run them ... that's what they are. So that's what you'll get. Hopefully the new people at Silverstone will look at it a lot differently. It's sort of grown out of a gentleman's club, which is now devoid of gentlemen."

No prizes for guessing who he was referring to. The BRDC, of course.

Bernie always knows that, in any business, there is going to be another chance, a fresh opportunity, to get his way. Nothing gets him down. "I don't worry about anything," he says frequently. Thus in December 2004, when Mr Justice Andrew Park delivered a High Court decision that one might have expected to elicit a trenchant response from the 74-year-old F1 commercial rights holder, it was almost water off a duck's back. Mr Justice Park said that the banks that then owned Ecclestone's business should have a say in how it is run, a ruling that could theoretically have challenged Bernie's control of the £415 million annual income generated by the F1 conglomerate.

Yet Bernie's response was simply a wry shrug, a mere twitch of a smile, and a knowing glance. He appeared no more concerned than if he'd been told that his Maybach limousine had been clamped by a parking warden. In fact, he looked considerably less annoyed.

"Don't ever make the mistake of underestimating Bernie," said Niki Lauda, the three-times world champion who left Ferrari at the end of 1977 to join the Ecclestone-owned Brabham team. "He probably knew before the court case started that he would probably lose. He is the perfect businessman who knows you just have to ride out the short-term ups and downs of this game. All his enemies may be happy and laughing, but they'd better enjoy it while they can because they may be crying soon."

On a personal note, Lauda added, "He's a great guy to work for if he respects you. It was very nice to drive for Bernie at Brabham, but it was simply impossible to negotiate with him. I had a big fight over the terms of my contract in 1979. We had one hell of an argument, but in the end he paid up. But that's the thing about Bernie. He will fight his corner ferociously, but once he's either won or lost he doesn't dwell on it. He just gets on with the next thing and relations are back to normal."

Ecclestone's impassive public demeanour masks a burning competitive spirit. He's not just a businessman. He is a racer. A straightforward businessman may take risky decisions, but racers such as Ecclestone live right on the edge. And just as in the days when he owned the Brabham team, he wants to have his finger on the pulse of every aspect of the operation.

He could be a difficult employer, insisting that the race preparation shop at Brabham should be kept as tidy as possible.

Sometimes he would pick up a broom and do a bit of sweeping himself, but more often somebody would be in deep trouble if they did not get the job done to his high standards.

He once threatened to close the factory down if he found it left in an untidy state, lining up the entire workforce in the bay where the transporter was parked to give them a corporate dressing-down.

Bernie used to drive the mechanics mad if a sponsorship sticker was even slightly out of line on the rear wing of one of the cars. On one legendary occasion he ripped a phone off a wall because the staff kept replacing the receiver the wrong way around, so that the cord did not fall symmetrically one side or the other.

His attention to detail extended to Brabham designer Gordon Murray's drawing office. He had the vertical blinds on the windows locked in one specific position so that sunlight shone through at precisely the angle he wanted, no matter whether or not it helped Murray concentrate on his drawing board.

"Oh God, yes, he could be an interfering so-and-so," says Charlie Whiting, the FIA race director and safety delegate who was chief mechanic at Brabham when Ecclestone owned the team.

"He was always standing on the pit wall with a couple of stopwatches he didn't know how to work. Then he would lose track, mutter 'damned stopwatches', and throw them down. But yes, he did like to be involved."

In particular, Whiting recalls the 1987 San Marino Grand Prix, when Riccardo Patrese was running second in the Brabham BT56, "which was pretty good for a Brabham in those days. He needed new tyres, but Bernie wouldn't let him stop.

"Then his team-mate Andrea de Cesaris was getting frantic. 'I wanna come in; I wanna come in!' he was shouting over the radio. And Bernie was shouting, 'No, stay out; stay out.' And I'm going, 'Bernie, for Christ's sake, he's got to stop for tyres – they're screwed!' In the meantime Andrea was getting more and more emotional. Eventually he came in for tyres with about five or six laps to go, I think, went straight out again and immediately crashed the car because he was so stressed out by it all.

"So I think perhaps Bernie got a little more deeply involved than he should have done, but at the end of the day it was his bat, his ball and he wanted to play the game exactly as he saw it."

That has always been the way. In the 1950s Ecclestone made a fortune as a car dealer in south London and later expanded to smart premises in Bexleyheath, the area in which he had grown up after his family moved from Suffolk, where he was born. Even as a schoolboy he was buying and selling: pens, cakes, anything in demand. And he always wanted to be in control. "Delegation is the art of accepting second best" would become one of his favourite catchphrases.

Ecclestone's talents were quickly identified by Max Mosley, as long ago as 1970 when Mosley was team manager of the fledgling March F1 squad and Ecclestone was in the process of buying the rival Brabham team. They met at meetings of the emergent FOCA, which Ecclestone would use as the foundation for his expanding power base through the following decade.

"Bernie was an ace negotiator," Mosley remembered. "I learned all the tricks of the trade from him."

Ecclestone has gained a reputation for being a man of his

word. But you'd better listen carefully. Jackie Oliver, the one-time owner of the now-defunct Arrows F1 team, remembers how the teams tried to oppose his move to introduce refuelling in 1994 to spice up the television show.

"We were all saying we didn't want refuelling and anyway the refuelling rigs were going to be very expensive," says Oliver who, as a director of the BRDC, experienced Bernie's business technique again at close quarters when it came to negotiating over the British Grand Prix.

"So he [Ecclestone] said, 'Okay, I'll supply the rigs', and we all accepted that. The next thing was that we were invoiced for them. So we rang Bernie and said, 'We thought you were going to supply these refuelling rigs?' And he replied, 'I said I was going to supply them; I didn't say that I was going to pay for them.'

"So you have to pay close attention to his choice of words. He is a good compromiser who will leave himself negotiating room. But you have to listen to what he doesn't say as much as what he does." Oliver can not quite conceal a degree of admiration for the smooth and seamless manner in which Bernie seems able to steer almost any situation in his own favour.

Similarly, watching Ecclestone working the F1 paddock is like watching a priest presiding over his flock. He shimmers from team to team, his uniform of Emporio Armani white shirt, dark slacks, and black loafers unvarying from day to day. A touch on the shoulder, reassuring or intimidating depending on your status, a grin, a brief pause for a quick exchange of pleasantries.

Then off to the next appointment, busy, busy, busy, sharp eyes never missing a trick, but not indulging time-wasters, either. Only at the end of a long day at the race track might you see him relax at his favourite paddock motorhome, run by Austrian hotelier Karl-Heinz Zimmerman, exchanging jokes and gossip with his close cronies – including Niki Lauda, medical chief Professor Sid Watkins, or perhaps – at least until the end of 2009 – Flavio Briatore, controversial team principal of the Renault squad.

On a personal level, Ecclestone is a private man. He lives in a Chelsea mansion only a few minutes' drive from his offices in Princes Gate, overlooking Hyde Park. He surrounds himself with a tight coterie of trusted acolytes, many of whom have worked for him since the Brabham days. To them he will always be Bernie; he is Mr Ecclestone only on the most formal of occasions.

Ecclestone, his former wife Slavica, and their daughters, Tamara and Petra, have all the accoutrements that go with serious wealth: the private jets, the super yacht in the Mediterranean, and the luxury cars. Yet somehow Ecclestone manages to keep his image low-key, almost unobtrusive. It is a clever balancing act.

Moreover, Ecclestone is very much a hands-on operator. He knows his way through the byways and cul de sacs of the F1 world like no other. That in itself has been a wearing and protracted lesson that Silverstone has learned repeatedly over the years.

Ecclestone and Sir Jackie Stewart were as oil and water in their dealings with each other. But if the BRDC foot soldiers imagined that life would be easier negotiating with the F1 commercial rights holder after Stewart's departure, they were to be disappointed. Ecclestone continued to drive Silverstone as hard as he could, determined to make them improve the facilities and never allowing much in the way of compromise to enter into his negotiations.

By summer 2008 it was business as usual at Silverstone. It was midway through its contract to stage the British Grand Prix but Ecclestone and the BRDC were already locked in their latest bruising round of contract negotiations to resolve what might happen beyond 2010.

The arrival of Damon Hill as BRDC president in 2006 had triggered a subtle change of tone in the negotiations between Ecclestone and Silverstone. Hill is the sort of guy who ought to have a franchise for calming frayed nerves. There is a measured and reassuring quality about the 1996 world champion that made him the logical choice to succeed Stewart – so much so that he could be considered Jackie's 'anointed one', continuing the tradition that the outgoing BRDC president, if not directly nominating his own successor, certainly has a deeply persuasive influence in appointing that pivotal character.

Damon's father Graham drove for Ecclestone when Bernie owned the Brabham F1 team in 1972 and Damon remembers as an 11-year-old kid meeting Bernie, who was visiting the Hill family home at Shenley with Carlos Pace, the brilliant Brazilian driver after whom São Paulo's Interlagos circuit is named.

But none of this gave Damon or the BRDC any preferential treatment when it came to honing the rough edges off the new contract for the race, which, it was speculated, might cost $23 million a year – plus inflation – from 2010. That said, perhaps there was an implicit sense of mutual respect and understanding between Hill and Ecclestone that restrained Damon from rocking the finely balanced boat as energetically as some of his colleagues might have liked him to during the early years of their business relationship. Damon's strategy was probably the right approach for the right moment. He was feeling his way. And rightly so.

Talking to Hill during the run-up to the 2008 British Grand Prix, I asked him about rumours that Ecclestone was interested in opening negotiations to move the race to Donington Park at some point in the future. This prompted only a flicker of a smile. But he picked his words carefully, neatly side-stepping the issue and instead offering some observations on the much-discussed prospect of government financial support being offered to help the race survive. Little did we know that we were literally only days away from the seismic announcement that Donington was to be the new home of the most important motor race in Great Britain.

"I think we're in an interesting phase in terms of the whole recent history of F1," said Damon. "I think the notion that F1 will achieve recognition in financial terms from the British government is fanciful. I just can't see any way that the government can pay directly to support a sport like F1 from British taxpayers' money and, indeed, I find it difficult to get my own head round it. But I can see more of a case for supporting somewhere like Silverstone as a state-of-the-art F1 circuit.

"I think there is a political problem in investing in F1 if it could be construed that this would go to private equity. I think there would be outrage. Add the fact that the FIA is a bit of a controversial organisation at the moment, which makes the whole issue even more of a hot potato.

"I think what we're trying to do at Silverstone is fulfil some of the government's ambitions for education and tourism by using the circuit's global brand to boost those initiatives."

Of course, the sooner Bernie inked a deal, the sooner the BRDC could get on with building the new pit and paddock area down on the exit of Club corner. "It actually doesn't work rebuilding the old pits, because that would put the track out of action for too long," said Damon. "I think there will be better viewing facilities down at Club.

"Bernie likes the plans, but he has to achieve his financial targets. In order for it to succeed there has to be a means of accessing more revenue, because as things stand now most of the income goes into the fee to Formula One Management.

"I think it would be much better, and Bernie would get what he wants, if he was to support us publicly. He is acquisitive and I understand that. Now you could argue that the BRDC is the only promoter who is looking at the whole thing rationally, in the sense that we have an obligation to guarantee the continued health of Silverstone and in the end there must obviously be a limit as to what we can pay. But at the end of the day you have to say that the British GP is one of the jewels in F1's crown."

There was another point to be made, as well. Damon Hill felt that it was all very well to be holding up the emergent new races as examples of what Ecclestone would ideally like to see at established European venues, but the inherent prestige attached to F1's global image and sense of history had been shaped not by Bahrain, Abu Dhabi or South Korea, but by Silverstone, Monte Carlo and Monza. The reason all these new venues wanted to climb on to the F1 bandwagon – and the reason it was such a commercially attractive proposition – was at least in part down to the groundwork that had been done for many decades by the historically significant events that had been on the world championship schedule from the very start of it all in 1950.

Under the circumstances, Damon continued, it was only logical that there should be some sort of premium benefit for these bedrock races that had done so much to make the sport what it had become today. In other words, Silverstone and the other established tracks should not be lumped together with the new venues, but given due acknowledgement of their crucial status. And if that meant not being screwed until the pips squeezed out by the F1 commercial rights holder, then that's the way it should be.

Damon was also fully aware that the jewel – Silverstone – would take on an added sheen if it delivered another British winner, which it duly did in 2008 in the form of Lewis Hamilton in the McLaren. He made no secret of the fact that he was a huge fan of Lewis, believing that the young British driver has all the qualities that go to make up a truly great F1 competitor. But a wry grin spread across his face when we touched on the tensions that seemed to have developed between the young McLaren driver and the British media.

Hill recognised this process as what might best be described as an inevitable rite of passage. "It's a bit like a cat with a mouse, isn't it?" he grinned. "I'm not saying that the cat wants to kill the mouse, but it's a test they put you through.

"It starts with the fulsome praise, and before you know it you've suddenly changed into a national embarrassment. I was talking to one of the tabloid journalists about this and he said, 'But Damon, you never went through what Lewis has suffered', and I replied, 'Hey, I was the one who was referred to as "prat" right round the front of *The Sun*.' And it was a quote from my team boss Frank Williams and, I can tell you, that sort of thing kinda hurts."

He added, "The real competitor motivates himself. All I wanted to do was achieve the results and you just need to ride out what the media is saying about you. That's what Lewis has to do. You just have to keep a sense of humour about it, although I must admit that I had sense of humour failure on many occasions."

Yet Hill felt Lewis could ride the inevitable storm with no problems. "I think he is fully prepared for success and has that slightly messianic focus in his psychology which spells out the fact that motor racing is his life and what his life means," he said.

"The only potential danger is that he expects there will be nothing but praise, because that's just not going to happen, and that's quite difficult when one day you're being hailed as the star who can deliver what Britain wants in sporting terms and the next day people are saying it was all an illusion." Naturally, winning the British Grand Prix in 2008 was sure to guarantee Hamilton hero status. "Of course," said Damon, "and Lewis knows that. No racing driver wants to finish second. He will be a British winner and then he'll get the whole kit and caboodle."

By this time in Silverstone's history, one of the F1 community's most enduring music hall gags was that the only two things you could be sure about for the British Grand Prix were the traffic jams getting into Silverstone and the fact that Bernie Ecclestone would use the occasion to blast the BRDC.

The 2007 British Grand Prix had almost totally followed the established script. Those of the 85,000-strong crowd who failed to set their alarm clocks for an early hour found themselves condemned to an hour-long queue along the A43 from Towcester despite recent investment in the much-improved road system around the circuit.

Those who fumed in the queue will not have known that the cause was the closure of some car parks due to the recent torrential rain, combined with the financially hard-pressed organisers seeking to trim the reputed £500,000 fee demanded by the local police authority to oversee traffic management arrangements. Yet it fell to Ecclestone to offer his customary bleak threat that the race would be scrapped after 2009 if his demands for a major circuit upgrade were not complied with.

"It hasn't changed anything, has it?" said Ecclestone dismissively in response to suggestions that Lewis Hamilton's emergence as an F1 force would have helped to guarantee the race's future. "Maybe they [the BRDC] will be able to wake up and think they can make things work and do something."

He also responded coolly to the view expressed by Damon Hill that the club hoped to obtain planning permission for the changes needed by the end of 2007, deeming that to be too late. "We've had a contract in place for five years. They've known for five years exactly what has to happen," he said. "By mid-2008 we've got to have the new buildings and everything put in place. I hope they've had a wake-up call and I hope they do something."

Against the precarious backdrop of its financial commitments, the BRDC had continued to do its level best to invest as much as possible in terms of upgrading the facilities, yet still struggled to correct the image of peeling paintwork, muddy car parks and overflowing toilets.

The Paddock Club may have continued to pander to the high rollers, but to venture into some of the dusty, rutted and neglected public areas behind the main grandstands on the start-line straight was still like entering a no-go area. It was easy to conclude that Ecclestone's punishing fees – and the lack of financial support from a government prepared to invest billions in the 2012 Olympic Games – ensured that the everyday motor racing fan continued to get the thin end of the deal.

In fact, Ecclestone went further. He signalled that he no longer wanted to negotiate with the BRDC and would work on a new deal to guarantee the future of the race only if it gave up all responsibility for running the event.

His comments seemed designed to increase pressure on the BRDC to finalise a new commercial structure and upgrade the circuit facilities at a cost perhaps as high as £30 million while it worked to maintain a place for its fixture on the calendar in the face of competition from new government-backed events such as South Korea and Abu Dhabi, which were on course to join the world championship schedule over the next few years.

"I want to deal with a promoter, rather than the BRDC," Ecclestone told *Autosport* magazine. "It is too difficult with the BRDC because you get no guarantees with them. We've said that unless they can get the circuit to the level expected from so-called third world countries, we are not prepared to do a deal. They know what we want them to build."

Silverstone had also by then revealed its so-called master plan, designed to create new businesses and finance the redevelopment of the circuit. A new pit and paddock complex, either built on the site of the current one or between Club corner and Abbey Curve, was also regarded as a compulsory requirement if Silverstone was to have a chance of holding on to its F1 race.

Ecclestone also hinted that he felt it was about time the British government got behind the grand prix with direct financial help.

"It is nice to have a British Grand Prix because it is the home of F1," he said. "But a lot is being spent on the Olympics. Perhaps they need to spend some money on F1."

For its part, the BRDC moved quickly to defuse any possible row that might break out as a result of Ecclestone's loaded observations. "Bernie is right in principle," said Stuart Rolt, the BRDC chairman. "We recognised a while ago that it is difficult for him to deal with the BRDC due to the complex nature of our ownership.

"We now have a small, independent negotiating team with all the right commercial experience to be responsible. We are going to make strenuous efforts to keep a British Grand Prix in the future.

"Bernie has seen the master plan, but we are in the hands of planning and that's when there could be changes later in the year. We also have the backing and endorsement of the minister of sport, Richard Caborn. However, this major project is very real and a massive amount of work is going on behind the scenes nationally and locally to make it happen."

Rolt continued, "We know what Bernie wants and that's the same thing as us. We keep him abreast of all that is going on and, as usual, our managing director Richard Phillips will be talking and meeting with Bernie on a regular basis."

Getting this far, in truth, had been a considerable achievement for the BRDC. Whenever the issue of how Silverstone was going to be improved, enhanced, and expanded came up for debate among the members, you could be sure of finding as many opinions and views as there were people qualified to vote on them. Being a members' club, it was understandable that members' privileges loomed large in many people's priorities – most notably the members' camp site, which had assumed the character almost of a religious relic among a handful of hard-core members, its defence always being mounted with the sort of ferocity more associated with the fight back to Dunkirk.

"The moment the camp site is mentioned, that's when I go on to autopilot at any BRDC members' meeting," one respected associate member told me early in 2010. "I know exactly which two members are going to be first to their feet, leading the charge, and a feeling of déjà vu surges over me." Good manners and personal loyalty forbid me from naming the individual who demonstrated such razor-sharp powers of observation, but he's certainly not alone with his reservations.

Throughout the first decade of the new millennium, the speculation over a possible home for the British Grand Prix never let up. Perhaps the most extraordinary suggestion came from Ken Livingstone, London's mayor, who went on record to the BBC with the assertion that London could conceivably host an F1 street race as early as 2007. This suggestion was made after an impromptu demonstration of eight contemporary F1 cars through the West End in the run-up to that year's British Grand Prix.

Given most people's perception of Mr Livingstone as a dyed-in-the-wool socialist, one might reasonably have expected him to start manning the barricades in blood-soaked opposition to such a capitalist sport strutting its stuff through the streets of the capital. This, remember, was the man who presided over the congestion charge and the recalibrating of London traffic lights that made the very concept of trying to take a car into the city a migraine factory of the first order.

Yet 'Red Ken' seemed swept along with the excitement this demonstration unquestionably generated. "We started talking to Bernie Ecclestone and his people about a year ago about putting on a proper F1 race," he claimed. "It would probably bring two million people to London and we're really up for it."

Livingstone added that he backed the idea and shrugged off claims it would cause too much disruption. An estimated 50,000 people had crammed into the capital to watch eight F1 cars drive on the impromptu course, but the event had to be cut short because of the large number of people attending.

However, he expressed total confidence that the capital could easily handle the organisation required for such a race. "Bear in mind that 85 per cent of the people who come into central London come by public transport," he told Radio 5 Live. "These things can be easily managed as long as you plan properly and nobody ever questioned Bernie Ecclestone's planning abilities."

He continued to explain that he had already "pencilled in" a possible route for the track, which would "centre on Hyde Park Corner and Park Lane", and said, showing a knowledge of F1 issues that came as something of a surprise, "Something like this takes a minimum of 18 months' planning, so you're most probably talking two years away." He also conceded that although Silverstone had a contract in place to host the British Grand Prix until 2006, there had been inevitable speculation that the London race could be held in addition to the existing event.

The idea certainly won the approval of all the drivers taking part in the demonstration, with Nigel Mansell, who was guesting at the wheel of a Jordan, reflecting the positive views of Jenson Button and Juan Pablo Montoya, both of whom believed it would work well.

"It would be awesome," said Montoya, who relished squirting his Williams-BMW down Regent Street at full blast. "I've raced on a lot of street circuits in America and they test the teams and drivers more. To bring F1 to people [here] would be a really good thing. People would get a better image of what Formula 1 is. A lot of people love it and a lot of people hate it, but on TV you do not see how extreme the cars are. It does not look that fast. But when you go and see it up close, it's like 'phew!' It's a different story."

Mansell added, "They have the infrastructure here and they have the organisation. It could be absolutely sensational. Look how quickly it has been put together. I reckon a circuit could be ready within one year."

As demonstrations in the streets of London went, this was the most unlikely in living memory. The 'track' ran from its starting point in Waterloo Place, at the bottom of Regent Street, via Piccadilly Circus through into Regent Street, up to the D.H. Evans department store, right through the pedestrian precinct outside the London Palladium, on to Marlborough Street, opposite Liberty, and then back on to Regent Street for the run down to Waterloo Place.

Eight teams sent cars to the demonstration, with Mansell, who retired in 1992, driving a Jordan and fellow ex-driver Martin Brundle in a Jaguar. Montoya, McLaren's David Coulthard, Button of BAR-Honda, Ferrari test driver Luca Badoer, Toyota's Cristiano da Matta, and Minardi's Zsolt Baumgartner all drove their regular cars.

It was certainly great theatre and there was little doubt that it had been a great spectacle attracting a great deal of spectator interest. The reality, of course, dawned very much like a cold shower the following day. It was almost impossible to envisage how such a race could really be initiated and the notion that great swathes of central London could be disrupted for the three weeks minimum it would take to lay out the track, erect the appropriate barriers, and generally ensure that all the necessary support services were in place seemed fanciful in the extreme. As event organiser Harvey Goldsmith admitted, there would be a number of bureaucratic obstacles to overcome before a London grand prix could get off the ground.

Of course, as yet another stick with which to beat the BRDC around the head, the London demonstration was a tactical success. It attracted huge media coverage and the romantic notion that the streets of Mayfair might somehow be transformed into the Monte Carlo of northern Europe must have set hotel owners in the capital salivating out of control. Certainly, the issue preoccupied one of the monthly BRDC board meetings that summer.

The more you scratched the surface of the London grand prix idea, the less likely it seemed to happen. There were secondary practicalities to be considered that nobody seemed to have addressed with any conviction. Central London's traffic is pretty well logjammed at the best of times and turning that upside down was a task that nobody was going to take lightly. But there was also the question of where the track-side barriers were to be acquired from and where they could be stored during the intervals between races.

It was a nice idea, but it wasn't going to happen. But the

issue of the London grand prix was to prove a fleeting diversion from Silverstone's main priority of retaining the UK's world championship-qualifying round. Within another couple of years there would be yet another rival venue spoiling for a fight over that privilege. And it was one that had far more inherent credibility.

CHAPTER SIX

DONINGTON PARK ENTERS THE EQUATION

How one schoolboy's dream was realised with a single F1 race in 1993,
Tom Wheatcroft proving that who you know was, in this instance,
almost as important as what you could manage to pay. Ayrton Senna
wrote a glorious page of F1 history, but repeating that achievement
would not be quite so simple.

Ever since Donington Park staged the 1993 European Grand Prix, thereby realising the life-long ambition of circuit owner Tom Wheatcroft, there had been a nagging feeling that Tom would really like to find a way of transferring the British Grand Prix to the circuit near Derby on a permanent basis.

It was, if you like, one of the great talking points of the British motor racing community. Anybody involved in UK motor racing who had any soul simply loved Donington and its roly-poly, gregarious owner Tom Wheatcroft.

When it came to motor racing, Wheatcroft was a romanticist, but an unusual one. Whereas most such individuals lack the hard cash to bring their dreams to fruition, Wheatcroft most certainly had the resources to make dreams come true.

Beneath that avuncular and gregarious exterior there lurked a razor-sharp business brain that had built up a thriving and prosperous construction business in the Leicester area in the years after the Second World War.

Wheatcroft was a passionate fan of the sport that had shaped his life ever since, as a teenaged schoolboy, he cycled to Donington Park to watch in wonderment as the 1937 and 1938 grands prix took place. Just over 30 years later, Wheatcroft, who never lived more than a few dozen miles from Castle Donington and was by now a millionaire, paid a reputed £100,000 to purchase part of the 1,100-acre Donington Hall estate, including the old race track.

Once the deal was done, the first thing Wheatcroft had to do was clean up the place. Donington had been pressed into service during the war as one of the country's biggest military vehicle storage depots and it would not be until 1977 that the track, albeit much shortened from its original configuration, was reopened for business.

The Donington Collection was also duly opened and became possibly the most remarkable motor racing museum in the world, home for many years to Bernie Ecclestone's collection of Brabham F1 cars. Wheatcroft and Ecclestone became close friends, dealing historic racing cars over the years, and, eventually, on Easter Sunday 1993 Wheatcroft realised a life's ambition when Ayrton Senna's McLaren won the rain-soaked European Grand Prix on his beloved track. It was 55 years since the teenager had stood in the spectator area watching his great hero Tazio Nuvolari winning the Donington Grand Prix in an Auto Union. Wheatcroft later confessed that the race had lost him £3 million "but it had been worth every penny!"

Wheatcroft was also a passionate enthusiast for entering his own contemporary racing cars. In 1970 he backed British driver Derek Bell's assault on the prestigious European F2 trophy, the key feeder series to F1, buying him a new Brabham BT30 and entering it under the Wheatcroft Racing banner. Bell had a great season with this car, finishing second in the series behind the more powerful Italian Tecno driven by Clay Regazzoni, who had just been promoted to the Ferrari F1 team.

Bell had a high regard for Wheatcroft, who stepped in to save his career at its lowest ebb at the end of 1969.

"By the middle of the summer of 1969, I was getting a bit desperate," recalled Bell. "The Ferrari deal just seemed to have drifted away, but Tom was obviously a great enthusiast and said, 'Lad, if I can ever be of any assistance, I would love to help you.' I didn't think a lot about it at the time, but the Ferrari deal turned out to be such a disaster that I began to think about doing the Tasman Series [a prestigious single-seater series in Australia and New Zealand] again the following winter.

"So when the chance came up to buy an ex-works Brabham BT26A, we got in touch with Tom and did a deal. Unfortunately we had a couple of engine failures in the Tasman Series, so I thought that was the end of the story for my career, but Tom came to my rescue again. We ordered a Brabham BT30 and ran it from Church Farm (my family base in Sussex). It was a classic season, which was rounded off when Tom loaned us a DFV engine to put in a works Surtees, driving which I scored the only F1 world championship point of my career in the 1970 US GP at Watkins Glen.

"Tom Wheatcroft had been a terrific supporter and he even dusted down his old March 701 for me to drive in a couple of non-championship F1 races at the start of the 1971 season, which I much appreciated. He was a huge enthusiast and I think everybody in British motor racing had a lot of sympathy with what he was trying to do in reviving Donington Park. He had great passion for the sport. He was tough but fair and always trying to help out."

Tom subsequently backed the determined young rising star Roger Williamson, who won the 1972 British F3 championship at the wheel of a Wheatcroft Racing GRD. They moved up into F2 at the start of the following year. Williamson won the prestigious Monza Lottery race in the Wheatcroft March-BMW, then Tom was persuaded to back him at the wheel of a works March 731 in the British Grand Prix at Silverstone in 1973.

Wheatcroft would also remember appreciatively the way in which Bell complimented him on backing Williamson. "He said to me, 'By God, Tom, you've got a fast lad there.' It was very nice of him. Drivers rarely compliment another driver and I appreciated that."

Williamson was eliminated from the race in a spectacular multiple-car accident triggered by Jody Scheckter's McLaren at the end of the opening lap, but was back in the cockpit for the next race, the Dutch Grand Prix at Zandvoort, where he was killed in a fiery accident.

Wheatcroft was bereft. He regarded Williamson almost as a member of his own family and, at the time of Roger's death, there were negotiations going on behind the scenes to secure him a drive with the legendary Tyrrell team for 1974 as the successor to Jackie Stewart, who, unbeknown to all but a handful of F1 insiders, was planning to retire at the end of 1973.

Interestingly, Tom Wheatcroft's longer-term involvement in motor sport might have been different indeed if young Williamson had survived. Roger had a tremendous sense of loyalty and really wanted to stay with Tom to do F1 on a longer-term basis in their own private team.

"The truth was we had a contract to sign with Ken, but we had to keep altering it," Wheatcroft told my journalistic colleague David Tremayne. "Then Roger come up the office one morning and he were in my office all day and then came home and had a meal with me. Finally he said, 'Oh Tom, I'm worried. I'd like to stay with you and drive for you.'"

Wheatcroft was quite candid in his advice to the young man. "I told him that we'd only hold him back and that Ken had forgotten more than we'd never know. But we had a chat and rang up McLaren and ordered a couple of M23s."

In 1974 an M23 would carry Emerson Fittipaldi to the world championship – and James Hunt would duplicate that achievement a couple of years later. One wonders what the gifted young Williamson might have achieved in one of these cars running under the Wheatcroft Racing banner.

After Roger's tragic death, Wheatcroft busied himself with Donington Park and all the challenges involved in developing the Donington Collection, which would become a key tourist attraction in its own right.

By the time Donington Park reopened in 1977, Wheatcroft was no longer a race team entrant, preferring to concentrate all his efforts on building up his beloved circuit. Tom enjoyed a good relationship with Bernie Ecclestone and they did business together on many occasions, usually seeking out and acquiring significant historic racing cars that had been squirrelled away at some distant location in another country. Both self-made men, they instinctively understood each other's philosophy and way of doing business. Those close to Ecclestone on a day-to-day basis formed the opinion that Wheatcroft was one of the handful of entrepreneurs for whom Bernie had genuine respect and admiration.

The first formal test at Donington took place on Friday 15 April 1977, when the formidable Broadspeed Jaguar XJ5.3Cs, which were contesting that year's European touring car championship, were invited to conduct a test session on the revised, shortened 1.9-mile circuit.

The following week's motor sporting press was peppered with Leyland Cars advertising celebrating the memorable moment under the heading 'Cat let loose at Donington sets new lap record'. Tom Wheatcroft was understandably delighted.

"I bought it five and a half years ago. We started building and planning four and a half years ago; six months after that, they said, no, we couldn't do it!" Of course, these words were delivered by Tom through gales of laughter.

The drivers who turned out to test the Jaguars on that memorable day included Tim Schenken, John Fitzpatrick, Andy Rouse, and Derek Bell. Wheatcroft also took a ride in a road-going Jaguar XJS with Bell and asked his old friend candidly what he thought. "I think it's a very good track that blends speed with safety," replied Bell openly. Tom sat back in the passenger seat and grinned to himself with a degree of well-merited satisfaction.

But if Wheatcroft had thought his problems were over, he was wrong. On the Thursday before the first race was due to take place, track manager Ian Phillips telephoned the RAC to make doubly sure it had received all the passes necessary for its officials, only to be told the RAC had withdrawn the circuit's track licence.

In a telex to Donington, the RAC said, 'The RAC announced today that, with regret, it is unable to issue a licence for the Donington motor racing circuit. Counsel's opinion was received by the RAC today to the effect that there is no legal way that a footpath that intersects the circuit at two points can be either closed or diverted [and] it is a criminal offence to obstruct the footpath.'

As one might have expected, Tom Wheatcroft's lawyers swung into action on the Friday morning and, after an eminent QC discussed the matter with the RAC, the RAC duly announced, 'It is lawful to run an event for cars over a footpath so long as it is classified as a trial and only involves motor vehicles as defined by law. This law does not include racing cars.'

Ian Phillips later explained that steps had been taken to advise of a diversion to the footpath for this occasion, but as the procedure involved publishing the news in the London Gazette, which august publication had been on strike for three weeks, the announcement was not made.

Long before the circuit hosted its sole world championship grand prix of modern times, Ecclestone had proffered a helping hand to Wheatcroft when it came to organising the Gunnar Nilsson memorial event at the track in 1979. This turned out to be a sprint event for contemporary F1 cars, won by Nelson Piquet in the legendary Brabham BT46B fan car, backed up by a race for BMW M1 Procars and a demonstration by Juan Manuel Fangio in a pre-war Mercedes W165.

Nilsson, an affable Swede who won the rain-soaked 1977 Belgian Grand Prix at Zolder in a works Lotus 78, succumbed to cancer in 1978 after a long and painful fight. The Gunnar Nilsson Cancer Treatment campaign was initiated to raise funds to fight the disease and was administered by Ian Phillips.

Phillips, a close friend of Wheatcroft who had previously been the editor of *Autosport* and was later a member of the

Jordan F1 squad from its inauguration in 1991, takes up the story: "Starting from the beginning: the Gunnar Nilsson event was Bernie's idea presented to the directors of the campaign, who included David Mason, the Mayfair art dealer who was one of the leading campaigners for compensation for thalidomide victims, together with myself and three cancer specialists, in response to a request from us to have a non-championship race.

"This request came as a result of a conversation between Tom and myself. Tom had wanted Gunnar to drive for him in F2 after his F3/Atlantic success in the UK but obviously he went into F1. We then met up again when Gunnar drove a JPS Lotus with Tom on the side-pod to open the circuit in May 1977.

"This friendship led to the desire to do something for the charity. Mr E. organised the whole F1 and Procar side of it. Sadly, poor weather on the date precluded him from arriving by helicopter to witness it. His innovative thinking for this event inspired Mason and myself to get Fangio in the Mercedes on the same day, which, from memory, was actually the highlight of the meeting."

Phillips added, "Over the years, Mr E. and T.W. formed a very close relationship – and, having witnessed both at very close quarters, I'd say they were peas out of the same pod. The 1993 European GP was entirely a gesture by Mr E. to recognise Tom's dedication to the sport. Tom had stopped collecting cars at this stage but knew every cellar, barn, and loft around the world where something of value was stored or hidden. As I understand it, Mr E. is now the owner of all these gems which Tom helped to acquire for him."

Tom may have lost money on his European Grand Prix, but

Bernie had certainly gone out of his way to convince the competing teams that this was a race they ought to support. Study the photographs of Wheatcroft standing in the rain on the podium with race winner Ayrton Senna and you will see a smile of unbridled delight on the face of the circuit owner, who had kept faith with his own personal dream and finally seen it happily realised.

Many people within the British motor racing community had doubted that such a day would – make that *could* – dawn. After years of lobbying, romancing, and cajoling, Wheatcroft had finally realised his great ambition to bring front-line international motor racing back to the circuit he had loved with such a passion for most of his life.

For the tough building magnate, who shrugged aside the effects of a mild heart attack in the run-up to the event, it was the crowning moment of two decades' endeavour to revive the first of all the road circuits constructed in Britain. Now there was to be a glittering new chapter written into this story that began in 1933 but had effectively lapsed from 1939 to 1977, when the track had lain unused by the motor racing fraternity.

Unused but far from forgotten.

Even when plans for that grand prix at Donington Park were originally announced by the sport's governing body, many had remained sceptical. It had originally been intended that the teams should journey to Japan for an Asian Grand Prix at Autopolis, but when that fell through Bernie Ecclestone gave Tom Wheatcroft the green light.

"It was a magnificent feeling when they told me I finally had a grand prix," said Wheatcroft. "It had been very difficult because on the occasions I'd asked him [Ecclestone] if I could have a grand prix, he would say he would get me one, and every time he couldn't I could see his point of view.

"If there are 20 countries wanting a race, then it's very difficult to give one country two. I thought it would never happen sometimes, but they were very honourable, kept their word, and I got it."

It was an undeniably competitive field, with the battle for outright honours being fought out between Ayrton Senna's Cosworth HB-engined McLaren MP4/8 and the Williams-Renault FW15Cs of Alain Prost and Damon Hill. Friday practice was held in torrential rain and, although the weather turned up for Saturday qualifying, the deluge returned on race day. It was cold, bleak, and miserable for the spectators, although the dyed-in-the-wool fans found their hearts warmed when it came to the main business of the weekend as Ayrton Senna delivered a virtuoso performance of rare brilliance. Two weeks earlier he had won the second round of the 1993 world championship in superbly dominant style in front of his home crowd at Interlagos. And now he was thirsting for more.

"With all this rain, the conditions are completely different," said Senna, relentlessly and repeatedly working the theme that his McLaren gave away a huge amount of sheer power to the Williams duo in dry conditions.

In dry qualifying Prost squeezed on to pole ahead of Hill, with Michael Schumacher's Benetton B193B on the inside of the second row ahead of Senna's McLaren. But it would be different indeed when it came to the race itself.

It may have tipped down on the day, but visiting dignitaries who joined the relatively modest 50,000-strong paying crowd included the Princess of Wales, with Princes William and Harry, and King Hussein of Jordan, an old pal of Jackie Stewart, who was keeping a promise made to Wheatcroft several years earlier that he would turn out to spectate on the day Donington finally hit the big time.

It was wet and October-like as the cars went out for their half-hour race-morning warm-up, in which Hill was fastest by 0.8 seconds from J.J. Lehto's Sauber and two closely matched McLarens, Michael Andretti on this occasion only 0.03 seconds from Ayrton Senna, the acknowledged rainmaster. Prost, not surprisingly taking it easy, was 11th fastest.

After a display of many historic racers with Donington connections, including a mouth-watering Mercedes W154 that a beaming Tom Wheatcroft managed to spin into a sand trap, the contemporary F1 cars were duly lined up on the starting grid.

Senna seemed obviously upbeat and optimistic. "The power is less important," he said. "The performance differentials go away in such slippery circumstances, which is good for us. We need such conditions to compete – not just wet, but also to be raining. Water all around the circuit is what we need."

At the start, Prost and Hill accelerated away cleanly and forged into Redgate, the first right-hander, with commanding poise and confidence. Senna's challenge was momentarily blunted as Schumacher edged him up on the kerb to the left, opening a gap through which Karl Wendlinger was only too happy to insert his Sauber to take a fleeting third place. But Ayrton's blue touch paper was well and truly alight and what followed was possibly the most sensational opening lap in recent F1 history.

Momentarily wrong-footed by the Benetton, Senna dodged around the back of Schumacher to take fourth place as the two cars accelerated out of Redgate. He sliced past Wendlinger on the outside of the Craner Curves and forced his way past Hill as they climbed towards McLean's. Through Coppice, down the return straight, and through the chicane on to the new loop, Senna was now gobbling up Prost's advantage and, as they braked for the Melbourne hairpin, he slithered past on the inside to take the lead.

By the time he scrambled through the tight left-hander on to the start-line straight and slammed across the timing line, Senna was already 0.6 seconds ahead of his arch rival, with Hill hanging on gamely in third. Remarkably, fourth place was now the preserve of Rubens Barrichello's Jordan, the 20-year-old having capitalised on the misfortunes of others to head Jean Alesi's Ferrari, Schumacher, Gerhard Berger's Ferrari, and the remainder of the pack.

Senna was unquestionably in a class of his own. Although virtually the entire field was on rain tyres from the outset, it seemed clear that a dry line was emerging almost before the race had got under way – to such an extent that Ligier driver Martin Brundle was advising his pit over the radio that he wanted to come in for slicks at the end of the parade lap. As it transpired, Martin stayed out until lap six before becoming the first driver to make the switch.

Tom Wheatcroft's dream race was turning into a classic that would have found its way into the motor racing history books even without the context in which it was taking place. However, for Prost, in particular, this was turning into a psychologically trying affair. Although his Williams FW15C was notionally the

147

quickest car on the circuit, had the conditions been dry, it had even more of a performance deficit to Senna's nimble McLaren than even his worst nightmare might have suggested.

In fact, neither Williams driver's cause was much aided by the fact that a slight problem with the automatic gearbox down-change mechanism was tending momentarily to lock their rear wheels under hard braking, which made them even more tricky to handle in the treacherous conditions.

This prevented them from braking really late into the corners. Moreover, in anticipation of the track drying out fully, the Williams team removed the gurney flaps from their rear wings, which further reduced the downforce and made them even more precarious to drive in the wet.

At the end of a race in which Senna made no fewer than five tyre stops in the changing conditions, he won by over a minute from Damon Hill. They were the only two runners to complete the full 76-lap distance on the extended 2.5-mile circuit.

Prost finished a crushed third and Senna made the most of his absolute discomfort. "I am speechless, really over the moon," said Ayrton as he summed up. "I could not have dreamed of a result like this. At the start, I really decided to go for it before Williams had a chance to settle down. They do have technical superiority and we felt this was going to be the best tactic."

For Prost, any comment would have looked like carping, particularly in light of the tension that had existed between him and Senna ever since their fraught two years together as team-mates at McLaren in 1988 and 1989. Nevertheless, he made the mistake of ploughing through his misfortunes during the post-race press conference, Senna cruelly feigning sleep in the chair alongside him as the Frenchman droned on self-consciously.

Senna listened. Then, with perfect timing, he interjected, "Maybe you should change cars with me." The entire media centre got the point. We all appreciated that on this historic day of days, such a switch would have made no difference whatsoever to the outcome of the race.

The next chapter in Donington's story was unexpected, even considering the convoluted traditions involved in the negotiations surrounding the British Grand Prix. Unbeknown to many people in the F1 community, in February 2007 Tom Wheatcroft had paid a visit to Ecclestone's London office to discuss what seemed like a very real possibility that the British Grand Prix might move to Donington Park. Bernie received his old friend courteously and listened intently to what he had to say.

The purpose of Tom's visit was to brief the F1 commercial rights holder about two businessmen who had become joint chief executives of a new company called Donington Ventures Leisure Ltd (DVLL). These were Simon Gillett and Lee Gill. They had secured a 150-year lease on the circuit near Derby, reportedly for a sum approaching £30 million. They were now interested in upgrading the circuit and making a bid for the British Grand Prix contract from 2010.

During the two years that followed, there would be endless speculation to the effect that the DVLL initiative was somehow a front for Ecclestone, wanting to create a situation that would lead to his owning the freehold of Donington Park, or Silverstone, or both. There were also those who believed his hostility towards the BRDC was so intense that he was prepared to acquiesce in any business move that would result in Silverstone losing the British Grand Prix.

To reach such conclusions is to misunderstand the man. Bernie's obsession, if it can be described as such, is the art of the deal. He wants the best possible commercial outcome from any scenario, for himself and his companies. Emotion is stripped out of the equation. He may say things that some choose to interpret as aggressive and critical, but in most cases this is simply manoeuvring.

He also loves gambling. My favourite Bernie story in that respect goes back to the 1974 South African Grand Prix at Kyalami, a race that was eventually won by an Ecclestone-owned Brabham BT44 driven by Carlos Reutemann. On the flight down to Johannesburg, Bernie had been playing cards with John Goossens, one of the marketing guys for the fuel company Texaco, and Bernie mischievously agreed that one of his Brabhams would carry Texaco stickers during practice if he lost the bet.

You've got it: he lost the bet and one of the Brabham BT44s duly rolled out into the Kyalami pit lane carrying Texaco branding. This was hugely embarrassing for Goossens, who almost literally begged Bernie not to do it. The irony here was that the Texaco backing for the rival McLaren team had been one of Ecclestone's targets for the 1974 season and the appearance of Texaco identification on a car owned by one of McLaren's main rivals was understandably bewildering to the fuel company's top brass back in Europe.

Similarly, when his team's rookie driver Richard Robarts briefly complained that there was no indication of his name on the side of the car, Bernie said nothing but mentally filed it away in his memory bank. Come the non-championship Race of Champions at Brands Hatch a few weeks later, the second

Brabham was pushed out into the pit lane with 'Richard Robarts' in huge letters extending pretty much from the front of the cockpit back to the engine cover.

It was all rather embarrassing for the former British F3 competitor, but no Brabham driver would ever again complain to Ecclestone that he had not got any personal identification on the side of his car.

Fast forward more than a decade and Lee Gill and Simon Gillett found themselves working hard to get their own dreams off the ground for Donington Park. In that respect, one would have to say that DVLL in general and Gillett specifically seemed to have an almost reckless ability to look on the bright side. When they outlined their plans for the race they were determined that everything would be bigger, better, more lavish, and more unrealistically ambitious than any other circuit might contemplate.

Neither man had much in the way of experience in the motor sport business, but they were both very optimistic that they could make a plausible case for developing Donington as a credible home for the British Grand Prix. Yet from the outset it seemed that they were running hard to stay ahead of unfolding commercial events. The global economic depression looked almost certain to get in the way of their ambitious plans. But they ploughed on with great confidence.

Gillett claimed that his goal was not only to make the track sustainable but also to make sure that his customers enjoyed the experience and would return year after year. He said that the sport long ago lost sight of how to treat the public and needed to focus on that to develop in the future.

The biggest surprise in his grand prix plan was that there

would be almost no access to the circuit for private cars. Club members would be allowed to drive in but everyone else would have to use park-and-ride schemes. Many big events these days do not allow cars to drive right into the venue but motor sport has been slow to follow.

The idea may have been environmentally friendly and based on the fact that the roads around Donington are simply not capable of coping with the traffic flow. Gillett argued that parking away from the track and being whisked into the circuit on an efficient bus service was a much better option because people would be able to come and go much more easily.

It also seemed very helpful that the construction of a new East Midlands Parkway station on the main railway line between London and Nottingham, around three miles to the east of the circuit, was nearly complete when DVLL outlined its plans.

Gillett's scheme for fast trains from London would have meant that fans from the capital could be home after the race in two hours. At some grands prix, that would not get you out of the car park. In the longer term, there was, he claimed, a good chance that there would eventually be a permanent light rail service between East Midlands Parkway station and the airport next to the circuit. There was thus potential for this to be extended a little farther to serve the circuit, as well. It was all strongly imaginative stuff. But a touch difficult to treat seriously.

There was even a suggestion that it would be possible to negotiate a deal whereby East Midlands Airport might be limited to all but aircraft bringing fans and high rollers into the race meeting itself.

Put simply, DVLL had bitten off more than it could chew and it was obvious for all the world to see, but the fact of the matter was that the proposed deal suited Ecclestone, if for no other reason than that it was somebody else putting pressure on Silverstone.

Damon Hill confessed that he was not totally surprised by this turn of events. Rumours had been circulating for some months before the 2008 British Grand Prix that a Donington deal was being mooted. Eventually the bombshell was detonated over the Silverstone race weekend, with Formula One Management announcing that a long-term 17-year deal had been agreed for the 2010 race to take place at this new venue.

Not that the current Donington promoters were spared a foretaste of what might come their way if they failed to match up to Bernie's exacting standards. Even as the ink was drying on their contract, Bernie dropped the strongest possible hint that the British Grand Prix might cease to exist altogether if they did not complete their upgrades to the track in good time for the promised 2010 fixture.

Asked by an enquiring local radio interviewer whether he felt the redesigned Donington Park circuit would be ready on time, Bernie replied impatiently, "How do I know? I'm not a civil engineer, so you should ask the promoters." But he added that it was perfectly clear in his own mind what might happen if they did not meet their obligations.

"I would do what I would have otherwise done this week – gone and signed up with somebody else." By that did he mean he would take the race to another country? "Yes," he replied.

In that connection, Bernie suggested that there might well be a case for more races on the calendar. In 2008 there were

18 events, but that was due to expand to 19 when Abu Dhabi joined the schedule in 2009. Meanwhile, Bernie had been trying to persuade the competing F1 teams to sign up for 20 grands prix at some time in the near future.

Threatening to remove the British Grand Prix from the calendar would send shock waves through the F1 community, of course, but would also serve to reinforce Ecclestone's belief that the global demand for his world championship package is insatiable. He therefore reasoned that he could afford to be uncompromising in his negotiations with new promoters who, like those at Donington, were prepared to pay around $30 million a year for the privilege of hosting a race – almost $8 million more than Silverstone was paying at that time.

Not that Ecclestone's remarks were intended to offer any solace to the BRDC. He wanted the club to be left in no doubt that the gate had been closed in its face and was now firmly bolted and barred. Donington had got the deal and that was an end to it. Except, of course, that it wasn't.

"There is nothing they can do," said Bernie dispassionately. "A couple of days ago I signed a binding contract with the Donington promoters and I don't want to be sued by them." The slightly self-deprecating tone of this observation seemed almost apologetic, but it was a thin veneer of good manners designed to conceal the real message, which was that when Ecclestone signs contracts he has every intention that the other party involved will abide by their terms. The clock was ticking on Donington's grand ambitions.

Meanwhile, in the BRDC clubhouse, the great and the good of UK motor sport reacted stoically, acknowledging that they had been here before, suffering the brunt of Ecclestone's ire because of their continuing inability to reach a deal to secure the future of the race at their own circuit.

"I think it's fair to say that the BRDC is sanguine about recent developments and will be making a measured response to the issue in due course," said one senior member. "On the face of it, there is no way that the mathematics of the new Donington deal can possibly stack up."

He added, "This business has nothing to do with any perceived spat between Bernie and the BRDC. It's about nothing more nor less than maximising the cash flow through Bernie's businesses and CVC Capital Partners, who are investors in his companies. In Formula 1 everything is about money and nothing else."

So how was DVLL going to deal with the issue of raising the necessary funding to upgrade Donington Park? The mathematics seemed daunting. Informed sources suggested that it would cost at least £100 million to completely revamp the circuit to the level required by Ecclestone and the F1 fraternity.

Gillett and Gill planned to start realising their ambitions by raising £40 million from a debenture scheme similar to that used to raise around £800 million to construct the new Wembley Stadium, effectively offsetting debts to the banks against future ticket revenues. But even from the outset it looked like a long shot. The economic climate was not right, with corporate hospitality programmes increasingly being reined in across the entire sporting horizon. Neither did it sound particularly encouraging that Lee Gill left DVLL within a couple of months of the deals being signed, as did financial controller Peter Edwards. And PR agents Sidhu and Simon Communications withdrew from handling the DVLL account.

Gillett now found himself pitched on to the back foot to allay fears that Donington would not in fact be ready to stage the British Grand Prix and went to some effort to dismiss stories that Gill had walked out after a disagreement over the direction of the project and accusations that Donington's plans "were being devised on the back of a fag packet".

He moved quickly to offer soothing reassurances. "Everything is on track, as our plans will show when they are released for scrutiny," he insisted. "There are no daggers in backs and no disagreements. We have been through phase one of this project and now we are in a new phase that demands changes. Lee was part of my team as we crossed the line on this one, but he has now decided to go his own way and we wish him luck." It was not enough to calm the waves of adverse speculation, even though Bernie Ecclestone tried to sound upbeat and positive when approached for his comments at this time.

"We've a contract with them, which I hope they honour," he said. "I'm not even considering there won't be a race there."

CHAPTER SEVEN

A DREAM STARTS TO UNRAVEL

How an audacious and over-ambitious businessman tried to pull off the impossible. Simon Gillett talked big and was suffused with enthusiasm, but his efforts to take the British Grand Prix to Donington ended in failure and laid waste to a great race track.

There were wider concerns emerging about the viability of DVLL's basic funding. Majority control of the company was shared between Gillett and Paul White, a Monaco-based property developer. According to Terry Lovell, who researched the matter in some depth for his book *Bernie Ecclestone: King of Sport*, the company's accounts to December 2007 showed a loss of £12.7 million and debts of almost £70 million. In 2007 White had also reportedly provided a guarantee of £4 million to secure a bank loan of £16.3 million from the Anglo Irish Bank. It seemed a somewhat cavalier way of carrying on, but Gillett had at least convinced Ecclestone that he was in a position to pay the Formula One Management fee and agreed to produce the necessary letter of credit to back this up in September 2009. You had to admire his optimism, but surely the only real justification for his optimism could be that Gillett knew something the rest of the motor racing world did not. Unfortunately for DVLL, this proved not to be the case.

During autumn 2008, the Donington circuit operators

continued to be tripped up by a succession of minor setbacks that, projected forward, inevitably intensified speculation that they would eventually run out of time. The biggest of these came to a head in February 2009 when a dispute over alleged rent arrears owed to Tom Wheatcroft's company showed that DVLL owed £2.47 million, which dated back to the previous September.

On 23 April 2009, Wheatcroft & Son Ltd began legal proceedings against DVLL in Derby County Court seeking forfeiture of the circuit lease in addition to the rent arrears. Kevin Wheatcroft, Tom's son, stated, "We are still in communication with DVLL and hope there is a path forward, as the Wheatcrofts do not want to risk losing the grand prix for Britain, but on the other hand, money is owed."

This dispute ran in parallel with DVLL's efforts to obtain the necessary planning permission for the redevelopment programme that would transform Donington into the magnificent 'pride of world championship motorsport'. The North West Leicestershire District Council had received this planning application by early September 2008 and approval by January 2009 was crucial if Donington was to be ready on time.

Clearly anxious to see this jewel in the UK's motor racing crown putting down long-term roots in the area, a special planning committee gave its formal consent on 9 January. "I couldn't be happier," said Gillett, "and from tomorrow morning it's shovels at dawn and away we go." Yet this optimistic rallying call was quickly shown to have a hollow ring about it. By the end of June 2009, substantive civil engineering work had been started but it was clear that the clock was ticking towards the project's oblivion.

The work that had been done to construct a tunnel under the track had proved to be very much more trouble than it was worth. Its positioning completely upset what was left of Donington as a going concern for club racing and the track fell into a state of limbo. DVLL clearly lacked the funds to finish the work to F1 standards but had gone far enough to ensure that the existing facility was unable to continue its normal national club racing activities. Tom Wheatcroft, by this time, was battling severe ill-health and was no longer available to be in the absolute front line when it came to negotiations, although his family looked after their collective interests with a continuing passion and well-developed sense of responsibility.

The Wheatcrofts nevertheless held the whip hand when it came to forcing DVLL to pay up the money it owed to the family business. The planning permission granted to DVLL came with what's termed 'a statutory section 106', which carries a requirement to meet certain provisions and enter into various obligations. One of the main issues relating to section 106 in this case was the provision of a satisfactory traffic management plan. This plan required the counter-signature of Tom Wheatcroft as the owner of the Donington Park freehold, a means of ensuring that, in the event of a change of lease, the contract could be enforced against the freeholder. Wheatcroft rightly declined to sign until the issue of the unpaid rent was resolved.

The North West Leicestershire District Council's planning committee eventually had to agree a deadline of 30 June 2009 for Wheatcroft to sign the agreement. Steve Bambrick, the district council's director of planning, stated firmly, "If the agreement remains unsigned by the end of June, we have said that we will no longer grant planning permission and instead we will refuse planning permission." Eventually the Wheatcrofts received their outstanding payment, but it was clear that the debenture scheme was an absolute non-starter and Gillett's Donington dream limped on with much vague speculation and talk about how his refinancing plans were proceeding. What was clear, however, was that even though Ecclestone was trying to help him, there was no chance of the F1 commercial rights holder staking any of his own money in the project.

"The world of banking has changed," said Gillett. "The bank we were planning to work with at that point has decided they were not in the market anymore, so we had to go and find alternative banks and there are banks in the market for it and we are just working through the details on this."

Steve Bambrick was clearly getting worried about whether Gillett could complete the work at Donington Park in spring 2010 – absurdly late, one would have thought, for the necessary circuit inspections to be done in time for a race that summer.

"Delivering what needs to be delivered for July 2010 is achievable, but only just," said the local government official in a formal tone that somehow contrived to remain both respectful and sceptical.

"From my perspective, partly because DVLL are relatively new and therefore we have not had a long-standing relationship with them, and partly because of things which have happened in the last six months, particularly around the planning application and the 106 agreement, they haven't exactly got a glorious track record for delivering things on time. Purely on that basis, there have to be questions."

Suggestions that Silverstone had privately been tipped off that it should stand by to initiate an interim upgrade of its F1 facilities as a fall-back venue continued to be brushed aside by those involved.

"As far as we are concerned, the British Grand Prix is moving to Donington in 2010," said BRDC president Damon Hill. "What we now have to do is knuckle down and work to ensure that Silverstone remains a centre of excellence for British motor sport."

Of course, it was by no means all doom and gloom for Silverstone. In January 2009, Donington had sustained another direct hit to its reputation when it was announced that the circuit would be hosting its last British Motorcycle Grand Prix that summer. It may have been scant consolation to Silverstone, set against the main issue of the F1 grand prix, but at least the BRDC would have the satisfaction of taking this prestigious event from its biggest competitor.

Only a week after Donington had apparently received a major boost by getting planning permission, Silverstone had secured the two-wheeler classic after out-bidding its rival to sign a five-year agreement with Dorna Sports, the commercial and television rights holder for MotoGP. Donington had played host to the motorcycle grand prix ever since 1987, but with all DVLL resources firmly focused on the bigger picture there was always the strong likelihood of losing this event to Silverstone. At the time it looked as though the BRDC had secured only the consolation prize, but things would plunge downhill for Donington pretty quickly from that point onwards.

Simon Gillett commented magnanimously, "Given the need for a flagship event in 2010 to replace F1, we understand the importance to Silverstone of gaining the rights to MotoGP from a business perspective. However, since 1987 we have continually invested in MotoGP, emotionally as well as financially.

"We would like to wish Silverstone the best of luck with the required construction and all of the work involved in staging a top-flight motorcycle race and ask them to take care of an event that we have invested heavily in since we took it over with just 18,000 people attending each race.

"We are proud to have hosted the championship for 22 years and our continuing passion and enthusiasm for the sport will ensure that our commitment and dedication for staging this year's event will remain just as high.

"However, I'd also like to reassure the fans that we will still be staging world motorcycle racing at the highest level with our continued support of the Superbike World Championship.

"The ongoing growth of this burgeoning series with an ever-increasing number of manufacturers and British riders will help to ensure that it provides close and exciting racing that should attract support and interest to equal that of MotoGP in Britain.

"We are also continuing our support of the British Superbike Championship and two-wheel club racing – proving our dedication and commitment at all levels of the sport."

Silverstone hosted Britain's round of the motorcycle world championship between 1977 and 1986, after the Isle of Man TT was stripped of its title status.

Richard Phillips, managing director of Silverstone, said he was thrilled to see top-flight motorcycle racing back on the calendar, adding, "Silverstone is the UK's premier motor racing venue and we are thoroughly looking forward to hosting the world's premier motorcycle racing event from 2010. We have worked closely with Dorna Sports to bring MotoGP to Silverstone and both parties are extremely excited about the opportunity to take this world-class event to another level."

Unable to resist a sly dig at Donington, he added, "Silverstone is a unique UK race circuit, rich in heritage and unrivalled in terms of what we are able to offer fans, championships, and teams.

"The grand prix circuit offers a combination of high-speed straights and technical corners, presenting a real challenge to the riders, while the facilities for teams and spectators are second to none. The circuit is also recognised as being one of the most easily accessible in the world. All of these factors, along with Silverstone's vast experience of hosting world-class international events, contributed to MotoGP coming to Silverstone."

Meanwhile, the F1 drama continued to be played out, both in public and behind closed doors. Hill knew better than to rock the boat at this delicately balanced moment in the process of saving the British Grand Prix. Yet by summer 2009 he was sufficiently emboldened by the obvious dire straits Donington had found itself in to allow himself the luxury of a little speculation. Gently and without too much in the way of fanfare, he began to think aloud that Silverstone might end up going back to the negotiating table with Bernie Ecclestone, in a bid to revive negotiations to keep the race at its current home.

Nevertheless, Ecclestone kept up the pressure. He shrugged aside the notion that the British Grand Prix might be held outside the UK on a temporary basis in 2010, returning to these shores when Donington was ready for business in 2011. Whether the questioning on this issue was a genuine line of media interest or a Donington-sponsored 'flushing-out' exercise to test whether Bernie might be prepared to postpone the move to the circuit was difficult to discern.

Certainly there was absolutely no doubting his reply on the

matter. "It won't go overseas," he said. "There just won't be a British Grand Prix. We can't just suddenly put the British Grand Prix in France or Italy or somewhere." And he also seemed to put his foot firmly on the notion of a temporary return to Silverstone.

"The answer is no," he said. "We left there for a reason and nothing has changed since. They've had plenty of opportunities, the time and the money, but they have gone off on their own way, doing things the way they wanted things, so that's it."

Yet by the time the 2009 British Grand Prix was taking place at Silverstone, there were even more dramatically mixed messages to be discerned within the F1 community as the sport had another very determined attempt at self-destructing. Not only was there much sentimental reflection over the possibility that this really might be the final grand prix to be held at Silverstone, but there was also the possibility that the sport was about to be ripped apart by a breakaway grand prix racing series under the aegis of the Formula One Teams' Association.

Ironically, as Richard Williams pointed out in *The Guardian*, it was a Brazilian who most eloquently enunciated the feelings of the Silverstone public. "I've loved this place since I ran here in Formula 3," said Rubens Barrichello, Jenson Button's team-mate, shortly after securing a starting position on the outside of the front row of the starting grid. "I know they cannot change the weather, but that's England. It's fast and it's safe. Why the hell are they taking the race away from here?"

The race itself delivered a brilliant victory for Sebastian Vettel in the Red Bull-Renault ahead of his team-mate Mark Webber, with Barrichello taking third place, all three drivers reminding us just what a superb circuit this really was.

But on Friday night FIA president Max Mosley let it be known that, in his view, the endangered race might well return to the old Northamptonshire bomber base for the following year. "I think the chance of there not being a British Grand Prix next year is very small," he said. "My personal view – it's not for me to decide – is that it's highly probable it will be at Silverstone."

His words, uttered, as Richard Williams wrote in *The Guardian*, with a silky casualness, directly contradicted the frequently expressed opinion of the man who does make the decision. Ecclestone, his co-conspirator of 40 years, had repeatedly stated that his decision to give the race to Donington Park for the next 10 years excluded the remotest possibility of returning to Silverstone. Ecclestone had emphasised that if Donington's promoters proved unable to fund the £100 million-worth of work necessary to host a round of the world championship, the British Grand Prix would disappear from the calendar – for a year at least and perhaps forever.

However, Ecclestone informed a television reporter – as lightly as if he were passing comment on the weather – that the thing previously deemed an impossibility might indeed come to pass and Silverstone could be destined for a return to the calendar next year. 'Those who heard him,' added Richard Williams, 'promptly redoubled previous pledges never to believe a word uttered in the Formula One paddock.'

A senior figure at one Formula One Teams' Association team claimed over the Silverstone weekend that several circuits, including some of those currently on the official calendar, had been in touch with a view to taking part in the Association-led series. The problems of replicating the travelling infrastructure of race directors, safety car personnel, medical staff, scrutineers, special transport facilities, timing equipment, and results monitoring could "easily" be overcome. No major sponsor, he added, had been anything other than unreservedly supportive of Formula One Teams' Association's stand.

For supporters of Silverstone, it was worth noting with a degree of satisfaction that the 2009 British Grand Prix attracted a capacity crowd of 90,000 spectators even though their home heroes Jenson Button and Lewis Hamilton had disastrous qualifying sessions and lined up respectively sixth and on the back row of the grid for their home round of the title chase. This came only a fortnight after fewer than 20,000 fans had turned up at the Istanbul Park circuit for the three days of the Turkish Grand Prix. The message hardly had to be paraded in lights above Piccadilly Circus. It spoke for itself.

Donington Park had originally been given until the end of September 2009 to raise the £80 million required to finish the circuit and finance the first race, but when it came to it Gillett was allowed a few days' extension to complete the financing arrangements.

It was understood that a merchant bank was involved in attempting to raise a bond for £120 million from various wealthy investors, but Ecclestone had warned the previous month that he would take the race back to Silverstone if the funding was not forthcoming. In fact, information circulating in the City suggested that the dilemma facing Donington's bankers was now quite intense and they were almost reduced to 'cold calling' a list of high-net-worth individuals to see whether they might be interested in taking a stake in the action. Such as it was, or might turn out to be.

"They have got until the end of September to produce a bank

guarantee," Ecclestone was quoted as saying in the *Leicester Mercury*. "I'm hoping Donington can do all the things they must do. And if they can't, we will come back to Silverstone." A spokesperson for Donington followed that up by saying that they were unable to discuss financial issues and that an announcement would be made in due course.

Switching the race back to Silverstone might not have been as straightforward as it appeared, however. Although Silverstone was keen on inking a long-term contract with Ecclestone, it had little interest in signing for a single year in 2010 if the intention behind such an offer was to give Donington Park an extra 12 months to ready itself for its debut race. The BRDC believed that would make no commercial sense.

"If the Donington programme comes off, then, fine, the future of the British Grand Prix is guaranteed for 15 years, at least on paper," said Hill.

"But they still have to deliver the race, the circuit, and its infrastructure. It's not just a question of raising the money. If Donington does not happen, then you have to ask yourself what that says about the decision to look into it in the first place. And in those circumstances it would be nice to think that we could get round a table with [Formula One Management] and put to bed once and for all the uncertainty over the future of the British Grand Prix."

All of which brought one neatly back to one of the biggest problems bedevilling grands prix in Europe over recent years – the difficulty in raising the annual cost of these events, which, typically, have a price tag of around $18 million, linked to a 10 per cent annual escalator for the duration of the contract. Many new races outside Europe pay Ecclestone's company much more, with the organisers of the 2009 inaugural grand prix in Abu Dhabi reputedly paying close to $30 million for their first event.

Hill added, "I absolutely accept that for new 'fly-away' grands prix outside Europe there should be a premium cost, but, by the same token, these new races are tapping into the tradition of long-established races, like the British Grand Prix, which were in at the very birth of the world championship and have been part of the sport's staple diet ever since."

Yet Ecclestone's patience was clearly wearing thin. Repeatedly he bent over backwards to give Gillett extra time in which to complete Donington's funding arrangements. By September 2009 he was so concerned that he gave Donington a final 14-day period to prove that it had the financing in place and could actually get the building work completed in time.

Gillett had been in negotiations with Citibank about the £135 million bond issue since an earlier Goldman Sachs fundraising round was scrapped in April. The bonds, which would mature in 2016, were scheduled to pay an annual yield of 15 per cent in view of the high-risk nature of the project.

The earlier plan to raise cash by selling long-term debentures that would entitle owners to the best seats for the grand prix and other races, as well as 'money-can't-buy' opportunities, had been "put on ice" until the autumn.

A spokeswoman said the debenture scheme would still go ahead but was not now being considered as part of the overall sum required to overhaul the circuit and its facilities. The project had been dogged by uncertainty over financing and planning consent, but Gillett continued to insist it would come to fruition.

ABOVE: *Another royal visitor graced the British GP at Silverstone in 1994 when the Princess of Wales joined race winner Damon Hill on the podium.* (LAT)

BELOW: *Lewis Hamilton proves he is made from stern stuff as he splashes to a convincing victory in the 2008 race at Silverstone in his McLaren-Mercedes.* (LAT)

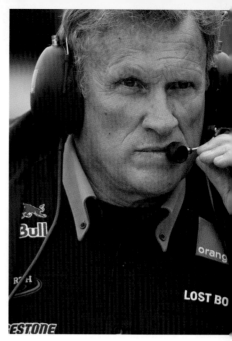

ABOVE LEFT: *Bernie Ecclestone has been one of the most powerful influences over the future of the British GP in his role as the F1 commercial rights holder, agreeing at various times that the race should go to Brands Hatch and Donington Park as alternative venues to Silverstone.* (LAT)

ABOVE RIGHT: *Tom Walkinshaw sold a share in his automotive retailing business to the BRDC, but the deal attracted strong disapproval from the club's membership.* (LAT)

BELOW: *Martin Brundle and Jackie Stewart worked well together in their respective roles as chairman and president of the BRDC, working to save the race for Silverstone.* (LAT)

ABOVE: *Nigel Mansell goes wheel to wheel with his Williams team-mate and rival Nelson Piquet on his way to victory in the 1986 British GP at Brands Hatch – the last round of the F1 championship to be held at the famous Kent circuit.* (LAT)

BELOW: *Nicola Foulston in her office at Brands Hatch. She agreed a deal for the British GP to go back to Brands Hatch and later attempted to buy Silverstone.* (LAT)

ABOVE: *(from left) Innes Ireland briefly held the position of BRDC president in the aftermath of the Walkinshaw affair. Lord Hesketh, seen with the BRDC president-in-chief, the Duke of Kent, also played a part in the negotiations for Silverstone to retain the race.* (both Sutton Motorsport Images)

BELOW: *(from left) Jack Sears stood down as president after the SMG discord (LAT); Ray Bellm fell out with Jackie Stewart during his period as BRDC chairman; Robert Brooks, chairman of auction house Bonhams, had taken over the role of chairman of the BRDC by 2010.* (both Sutton Motorsport Images)

ABOVE: *Stuart Rolt (left), whose father Tony won Le Mans for Jaguar in 1953, succeeded Ray Bellm as BRDC chairman. He is seen with Jackie Stewart and Damon Hill, former and current BRDC presidents respectively.* (LAT)

BELOW: *Prime Minister Gordon Brown presents Jenson Button with the Richard Seaman Trophy on the day Silverstone's deal for the British GP was confirmed in December 2009.*
(Sutton Motorsport Images)

ABOVE: *Ayrton Senna celebrates his victory in the 1993 European GP at Donington Park with circuit owner Tom Wheatcroft.* (Sutton Motorsport Images)

BELOW: *Donington Leisure boss Simon Gillett is all smiles with Bernie Ecclestone at Silverstone in 2008 when it was announced that the race would be moving to Donington in 2010 at the start of a 17-year deal.* (Sutton Motorsport Images)

ABOVE: *Gillett poses by a JCB earth mover as Donington prepares to make a start on its civil engineering works, but his optimism was soon to be dashed.* (Sutton Motorsport Images)

BELOW: *Donington Park looking like an abandoned building site after work on the redevelopment plans ground to a halt towards the end of 2009.* (LAT)

ABOVE: *The official inauguration of the revised Silverstone circuit on 29 April 2010, attended by (from left) David Coulthard, Mark Webber, BRDC president Damon Hill, HRH The Duke of York (UK Special Representative for Trade and Investment), the Bishop of Brixworth, the Right Reverend Frank White and Silverstone's Richard Phillips.* (Getty Images)

BELOW: *Jackie Stewart waves the chequered flag as Damon Hill finishes his high-speed run chauffeuring the Duke of York in a two-seater F1 machine.* (Getty Images)

"We have made great strides in recent weeks and greatly appreciate the additional time allowed to us to finalise the information for public distribution in what has been a much more difficult than anticipated economic climate," said Gillett as time began to run out.

"We appreciate the British public's growing frustration with regard to uncertainty that has been cast over the country's largest and most successful motor sport event, but remain committed to delivering on the promises that we made at the start of this process and have the interests of the sport and its fans at heart."

Ecclestone said that Donington had already failed to meet one deadline and was now technically in breach of the contract that granted it a 17-year licence to host the race.

He also prepared the ground to reopen negotiations with Silverstone's owners, the BRDC, if Donington failed to supply the necessary guarantees. As part of that process he promised the BRDC a long-term deal on similar terms to Donington's.

Simon Gillett's grand ambitions to hold the British Grand Prix at Donington finally fell on a weekend that was full of pathos and symbolism – that of the inaugural Abu Dhabi Grand Prix on the lavish Yas Marina circuit in the Gulf state.

Ecclestone delivered the news that Donington was finished as far as F1 was concerned to a group of media representatives in the run-up to the Abu Dhabi race, making the point that Donington had failed to meet the final, immutable deadline set for the previous Monday after DVLL's bankers were unable to generate enough interest in their £135 million bond.

"There's no Donington," he said firmly. "They've missed the deadline, which we kept extending for them. It's unfortunate for them, to be honest. It was the credit crunch that caused them to be in trouble because their intentions were good, that's for sure. It's bad for Tom, because he's been an old friend for a long time." Wheatcroft died only three days after Ecclestone made this rather wistful remark, at the age of 87 after a long illness.

Ecclestone also reassured the F1 fraternity that he was still in talks with Silverstone, insisting that there was no difference of opinion between himself and the BRDC. "We're talking," he confirmed. "A deal can be done if they want it to."

He also took the opportunity to praise just what a splendid job the Abu Dhabi promoters had done with their new circuit. "What they have done is unbelievable," he said. "It was in April 2006 I saw and spoke to the crown prince and that time we didn't start to discuss a race. But during dinner we came up with the idea that maybe we should have a race here and it's magic what they have done.

"I never thought it would be finished like this. I thought bits and pieces would be done. I said to them, 'I hope we're not going to be racing on a building site.' But no-one is going to top this, although I will be happy if someone does the same!"

On 18 November, just under three weeks after Ecclestone announced that the British Grand Prix would not be moving to Donington Park after all, the final nails were driven into the coffin of Simon Gillett's ambition with the announcement that DVLL was going into administration. The 40 staff employed at the circuit were given the news by Begbies Traynor, the business recovery specialist. Nigel Price, from the administrator, held out some hope that an overseas firm – unnamed at this stage – might be interested in taking over the circuit.

"This need not be the end of F1 at Donington," he said

optimistically. "It still remains a fantastic location, next to an airport and main motorway connections. It needs people of vision to get the dream to the starting grid.

"We have been made aware today of people who have the funding available and a keen interest in having F1 at Donington."

Price added that discussions would be held over the following few days and that the administrators were "very interested" in talking to other potential bidders. He continued, "We are certainly hopeful that a 2011 grand prix could take place at the site."

It also emerged that the staff at the track were not directly employed by DVLL, but worked for a separate company, which had not gone into administration.

DVLL's most recent annual accounts, filed at Companies House in February 2009, revealed a loss of £12.4 million and debts of £66.7 million. The company had a 150-year lease on the circuit from landlord Wheatcroft & Son Ltd.

Simon Gillett was unavailable for comment, as he had been since Bernie Ecclestone announced Donington had not been able to raise the revamp money. The main contractor for the revamp work, McAlpine, was also unavailable for comment.

Tim Parnell, one of the senior members of the BRDC, and the son of renowned former F1 driver Reg Parnell, is one of those who lives close by the Donington circuit and found himself swamped with mixed feelings after the initiative to revive the track stalled.

"The big question is: what happens to Donington now?" he mused. "Work had already started on the upgrade. The famous Dunlop bridge has been taken down and some parts of the circuit have been dug up. It's such a mess and it will need investment to get the circuit back to how it was."

His father took part in the first ever F1 world championship race at Silverstone in 1950, finishing third. He also went on to become a successful team manager and when he died Tim took over the reins, managing the BRM team until 1974.

He said, "I am very much involved with Silverstone, but I also have a lot of affection for Donington. My father saw his first race there in the 1930s. It was where motor racing started for our family, so I'm extremely saddened by what is happening now."

Tim said he had had his reservations when it was first announced that Donington had secured the British Grand Prix: "My reaction was, I'll believe it when I see it. It was just too huge a project to complete in such a short space of time." In that respect he was just one of many.

Finally, after a few weeks' more negotiation, Silverstone saved the British Grand Prix for the next 17 years, BRDC president Damon Hill confirmed on the morning of 7 December 2009. The newly signed deal has ensured that one of the most historic races on the F1 calendar retains its place in the sport.

Speaking at the press conference, Hill said, "It is not easy to enter into a contract of this magnitude and you have to take on a lot of responsibility, but the BRDC wanted this relationship to continue and we were prepared to back the negotiating team, with the level of risk satisfactory for the deal to go ahead.

"Everyone was well aware that the British GP is not just a sporting event, but it is a dynamo of the industry in this country. Losing it would have been damaging and perhaps there would have been no coming back.

"The title of Silverstone as home of motor sport has come true. It is a place for all motor sport. Everyone in the BRDC loves motor sport and we are looking forward to the MotoGP as well as the British Grand Prix."

Hill added, "This is tremendous news."

Under the terms of the deal Silverstone pledged to redevelop the pits and paddock at a new site on the exit of Club corner, although this work would not be completed until the 2011 race. Meanwhile, revisions to the circuit would go ahead in time for the 2010 race.

Bernie Ecclestone welcomed the deal, adding, "This will ensure the British Grand Prix is included on the Formula 1 calendar for many years to come, which is something I've always wanted. The team at Silverstone already know how to organise a good event and now everyone can look forward to next summer at Silverstone."

The original proposal from Bernie was that the BRDC should effectively take over a deal for the race on the same terms as had been tabled for Donington. But Silverstone's owners regarded this as still too costly and, after some further robust negotiation, a mutually acceptable deal was thrashed out.

BBC F1 commentator, and former F1 driver, Martin Brundle said, "It's brilliant news. I always assumed it would happen in the end because everyone wanted the same thing. The new circuits are exciting and interesting but they always had to balance up with the historic circuits, like Silverstone."

Silverstone managing director Richard Phillips added, "We've always had five-year deals and never been able to get the investment we needed to redevelop. But 17 years gives us the ability to invest and move forward.

"We've always had the belief the British Grand Prix was an important cornerstone of Formula 1 but, with Bernie, you're never quite sure. At the end of the day, though, you have to have a British Grand Prix."

Sports minister Gerry Sutcliffe was quick to welcome the announcement and said, "The news the British Grand Prix is to stay at the iconic Northamptonshire track will be welcomed by millions of fans – not just in this country but across the world."

Silverstone was due to stage the British MotoGP in 2010 on a modified track and planned also to use the revamped layout for the F1 race, as long as Silverstone officials could get approval from Formula One Management. If not, they planned to stick with the old circuit.

As the ink dried on the contract, so it was time to take stock.

MotorSport Vision boss Jonathan Palmer, whose company already ran Brands Hatch, Snetterton, Oulton Park, Cadwell Park, and its Bedford complex, admitted that he would be keeping an eye on Donington's future.

"I'd love to have Donington as part of the MSV group but I'm really not sure what Kevin Wheatcroft's plans are for the circuit yet," he told the *News of the World* early in 2010.

"I've not been up there, but we'll certainly be monitoring the situation and if they were interested in selling or leasing we'd certainly put a case forward, but it's pretty early days for that yet."

He was strongly critical of Gillett's handling of the F1 bid.

"Donington is a fabulous circuit and I think it's such a tragedy frankly that it's been messed up so much," Palmer said. "I'm afraid Simon Gillett's done that circuit no favours whatsoever. An awful lot of promises, very few of which ever came to anything.

"The legacy of it is a very despoiled circuit that needs a lot of work doing. It's not just work on the circuit to repair the false start on the grand prix development, but the general standard of it. Anyone [who's been there has seen that] the approach roads are very pot-holed; it's very tardy and shabby.

"It's not been looked after; there's been a hopeless lack of investment by the leaseholder in the last two or three years. But it really deserves some TLC and I hope whoever does take it over really does a good job on it because it really deserves it."

Bernie Ecclestone had previously suggested that DVLL's ambitions were ruined by the worldwide financial crisis, but Palmer said Gillett should have foreseen the problems.

"If I screw up MSV it's going to be my fault," he argued. "If Brands Hatch can't run next year, I've got to take the can for it. That's what being the boss is all about: you take the responsibility and the downside.

"The blame lies with Simon Gillett. He was chief executive; he made a lot of promises. You don't go into deals where someone says, 'Yeah, don't worry, I'll give you £50 million.' You just don't do that sort of thing on a casual basis.

"If people let you down, it's because it wasn't there in black and white and wasn't contracted properly in the first place. It's not easy doing it, but in truth Simon Gillett bit off far more than he could chew.

"It was a very ambitious project; it wasn't realistic. Most of us on the inside of motor sport knew that; few of us ever thought it was going to happen, but he continued to assert that it was and at the end of the day it hasn't, so we're not surprised."

Palmer added that he could see Ecclestone's logic in bringing Donington into the fray, but that he was pleased the race was ultimately returning to Silverstone.

"Bernie's business is getting the most amount of money he can for selling rights to a grand prix," he said. "The best way to make money for something is to create a market. If you've only got one circuit bidding for it, it's not a market. If you find somebody else that wants to do it, you've got a market.

"It probably did put a bit of pressure on Silverstone. I'm delighted it's gone back to Silverstone – it's the rightful place for it and I'm sure they'll do a good job with it. For Bernie, I doubt he thought it was ever going to happen [at Donington], but it suited his negotiation stance. But with Bernie you never quite know.

"The facilities at Silverstone are already better than a lot of other grand prix circuits. We were at Barcelona for Formula 2 and the paddock area and buildings were far shabbier than Silverstone is now. Silverstone has worked really hard in the last year or two to smarten that place up and I think they've done a good job."

Finally, early in 2010, Silverstone announced that it would use its new 'arena' layout for the 2010 British Grand Prix.

The revised track had originally been designed with MotoGP in mind, but when Silverstone regained its F1 date it began considering whether to switch F1 to the new circuit as well. It could now confirm that Formula One Management had approved the use of the layout.

"The new sections of circuit were initially brought in to comply with MotoGP safety regulations, but the 'arena complex' was always designed with both two- and four-wheeled racing in mind," said Silverstone managing director Richard Phillips.

"We have been very careful, working closely with drivers and riders, to make sure we are improving and enhancing what Silverstone already has to offer – from a driver's, rider's, and spectator's point of view."

The new circuit leaves the previous grand prix layout at Abbey and heads through an S-bend to the new arena complex, before returning down the national track straight to rejoin the grand prix track's stadium section at Brooklands. F1 cars will therefore no longer use Bridge and Priory corners, but the hope was that the changes would increase overtaking opportunities.

"Some will miss not seeing modern-day F1 cars accelerating through Bridge, but we have to move with the times and continue looking at ways to improve the overall experience," Phillips said. "The new layout will bring an extra dimension to Silverstone, a new challenge for the drivers, and will enable fans to get closer to the action.

"We have a very exciting year ahead of us, with F1, MotoGP, and world superbikes all coming to Silverstone, and I can't wait to see how the drivers and riders tackle the new circuit."

The revisions would add 760 metres to Silverstone's grand prix track and were expected to increase F1 lap times by around four seconds.

Ironically, BRDC president Damon Hill found himself slightly at odds with the concept of the new track layout. Always very much his own man, Hill described the £5 million redesign as "a frustrating compromise" that risked destroying the essence of what originally brought fans to F1 in the first place.

Asked for his thoughts on the biggest transformation to Silverstone's layout since it staged the inaugural F1 race in 1950, Hill said, "If you are asking me to say it's fantastic, I'm afraid I am not going to do that. I am not satisfied that we will be providing the best facility we could.'

By the time the track was ready to be officially opened by the Duke of York on 29 April 2010, Hill was striking a more positive note. "We think we have one of the world's greatest race tracks and we'll be fighting tooth and nail to keep it that way," he said. "Drivers have historically loved Silverstone and we hope we have designed a challenging, exciting track that will make them like racing here more than ever."

Both Hill and Phillips knew the redesign would help raise funds to meet the £300 million deal struck between Silverstone and Bernie Ecclestone to host the British Grand Prix for 17 more years.

Meanwhile, as lawyers and accountants picked over the debris of Donington Park, it emerged that finance and development experts brought in to help give credibility to Simon Gillett's F1 dream were among those damaged when the plans collapsed.

Finance specialist International Stadia Group was left with an unpaid bill of £103,500. The subsidiary of sports marketers IMG had helped source funding and sell premium seating at Wembley Stadium, London's O2 Arena (formerly the Millennium Dome), and Dublin's Aviva Stadium.

The company had been bullish in support of DVLL's plans. Speaking in June 2009, when problems signing off planning documents were finally overcome, International Stadia Group chief executive Andrew Hampel had said, "It is nonsense to say that the Donington Park figures and debenture scheme do not stack up.

"ISG has vast experience and we are world leaders in the area of stadium and arena marketing. Without doubt, as paying customers, motor sport fans are ready for the same level of quality that fans of other leading sports have become accustomed to and there is no reason that Donington Park cannot provide that."

An administrators' report has revealed that, when Hampel uttered those words, the company was embarking on its third finance bid, a bond issue, after two previous attempts to fund the project had collapsed.

Many of the biggest creditors of DVLL turned out to be firms offering professional and consultancy services associated with the project. The administrators' papers also showed that DVLL went into administration owing £3,100,000 in rent arrears to circuit owners Wheatcroft & Son.

Creditors of the subsidiary company Donington Park Leisure Ltd were much more numerous and were generally owed smaller sums of money. They included an £83,000 debt to Leicestershire and Rutland St John Ambulance and more than £78,000 owed to the local tradesman who helped maintain the grounds.

A total figure for the extent of the two companies' debts was difficult to come by, because the administrators' calculations include a liability owed to the Anglo Irish Bank that was listed separately against both companies, because they are jointly and severally liable for it. There is also no provision for the cost of the administrators' services.

The estimated deficiency as regards creditors given in the

directors' estimated statement of affairs was £18,260,655 for DVLL and £16,937,288 for Donington Park Leisure Ltd. But, once bank debt was accounted for, the amount actually owed to creditors was around £4.8 million.

As the business could not be sold as a going concern, the administrators' focus moved on to realising the best possible outcome for its secured and preferential creditors, including the Anglo Irish Bank.

The administrators were due to report on their progress within six months of the companies entering administration, or on exit from administration, whichever was sooner. They then had to chase any money owed to the two companies – including VAT refunds – and sell the plant, machinery, and equipment.

Poignantly, this meant the administrators' report was likely to be published at the height of the 2010 F1 world championship season, a few weeks before the British Grand Prix was due to take place.

At Silverstone.

RESULTS

1926, 7 August

BROOKLANDS, 110 laps of 2.616-mile circuit

1st, R. Senechal/L. Wagner (Delage), 4h 0m 56s, 71.61mph; 2nd, M. Campbell (Bugatti), 4h 10m 44s; 3rd, R. Benoist/A. Dubonnet (Delage), 4h 18m 8s.

1927, 1 October

BROOKLANDS, 125 laps of 2.616-mile circuit

1st, R. Benoist (Delage), 3h 49m 14s; 2nd, E. Boulier (Delage), 3h 49m 21s; 3rd, L. Chiron (Bugatti).

1937, 1 October

DONINGTON PARK, 80 laps of 3.125-mile circuit

1st, Bernd Rosemeyer (Auto Union), 3h 1m 2s, 82.86mph; 2nd, Manfred von Brauchitsch (Mercedes), 3h 1m 40s; 3rd, Rudolf Caracciola (Mercedes), 3h 2m 18s; 4th, H.-P. Muller (Auto Union), 3h 4m 50s; 5th, Rudolf Hasse (Auto Union), 3h 9m 50s; 6th, 'Bira' (Maserati), 78 laps.

1938, 22 October

DONINGTON PARK, 80 laps of 3.125-mile circuit

1st, Tazio Nuvolari (Auto Union), 3h 6m 22s, 80.49mph; 2nd,

Hermannn Lang (Mercedes), 3h 8m 0s; 3rd, Dick Seaman (Mercedes), 79 laps; 4th, H.-P. Muller (Auto Union), 79 laps; 5th, Manfred von Brauchitsch (Mercedes), 79 laps; 6th, A. Dobson (ERA) 74 laps.

1948, 2 October
SILVERSTONE, 65 laps of 3.67-mile circuit

1st, Luigi Villoresi (Maserati 4CLT/48), 3h 18m 3s, 72.28mph; 2nd, Alberto Ascari (Maserati 4CLT/48), 3h 18m 17s; 3rd, Bob Gerard (ERA), 3h 20m 6s; 4th, Louis Rosier (Talbot-Lago), 64 laps; 5th, 'Bira' (Maserati), 64 laps; 6th, John Bolster (ERA), 63 laps.

For this inaugural event at Silverstone the contemporary 1.5-litre supercharged cars were supplemented with a number of pre-war 'voiturette' machines to flesh out the field. Louis Chiron's Talbot-Lago started from pole as the two Italian Maserati drivers arrived late, missing the official practice session. But even though they started from the back of the grid they totally dominated the event.

1949, 14 May
SILVERSTONE, 100 laps of 3-mile circuit

1st, Emmanuel de Graffenried (Maserati 4CLT/48), 3h 52m 50.2s, 77.31mph; 2nd, Bob Gerard (ERA), 3h 53m 55.4s; 3rd, Louis Rosier (Talbot-Lago), 99 laps; 4th, David Hampshire/Bill Cotton (ERA), 99 laps; 5th, Philippe Etancelin (Talbot-Lago), 6th, Fred Ashmore (Maserati), 97 laps.

For the second straight year the field was dominated by post-war Maseratis, although Bob Gerard did an excellent job qualifying his ERA among the five-car front row of the starting grid. This time it was the Maserati of 'Toulo' de Graffenried who took the honours after the similar cars of 'Bira' and Villoresi retired, both having earlier led the race.

1950, 13 May
SILVERSTONE, 70 laps of 2.889-mile circuit

1st, Giuseppe Farina (Alfa Romeo 158), 2h 13m 23.6s, 90.96mph; 2nd, Luigi Fagioli (Alfa Romeo 158), 2h 13m 26.2s; 3rd, Reg Parnell (Alfa Romeo 158), 2h 14m 15.6s; 4th, Yves Giraud-Cabantous (Talbot-Lago), 68 laps; 5th Louis Rosier (Talbot-Lago), 68 laps; 6th, Bob Gerard (ERA), 67 laps.

With the British royal family turning out to spectate, this race went down in history as the first ever qualifying round of the recently inaugurated official world championship and the first time the classic 'Alfettas' competed in the UK. Fangio's Alfa damaged an oil line after thumping a straw bale, spoiling the symmetry of a potential one-two-three-four grand slam for the Italian team.

1951, 14 July
SILVERSTONE, 90 laps of 2.889-mile circuit

1st, Froilan González (Ferrari 375), 2h 42m 18.2s, 96.12mph; 2nd, Juan Manuel Fangio (Alfa Romeo 159), 2h 43m 9.2s; 3rd, Luigi Villoresi (Ferrari 375), 88 laps; 4th, Felice Bonetto (Alfa Romeo 159), 87 laps; 5th, Reg Parnell (BRM P15), 85 laps; 6th, Consalvo Sanesi (Alfa Romeo 159), 84 laps.

This was a memorable race highlighted by the victory of the 4.5-litre non-supercharged Ferrari over the thirsty, straight-eight cylinder Alfa Romeo. Crucial to González's success was a much shorter refuelling stop than Fangio's, allowing the Ferrari driver to build up a lead of almost a minute at the chequered flag. The BRM P15s – Britain's so-called national racing cars – finished fifth and seventh in the hands of Reg Parnell and Peter Walker.

1952, 19 July
SILVERSTONE, 85 laps of 2.927-mile circuit

1st, Alberto Ascari (Ferrari 500), 2h 44m 11.0s, 90.92mph; 2nd, Piero Taruffi (Ferrari 500), 84 laps; 3rd, Mike Hawthorn (Cooper-Bristol), 83 laps; 4th, Dennis Poore (Connaught), 83 laps; 5th, Eric Thompson (Connaught), 82 laps; 6th, Giuseppe Farina (Ferrari 500), 82 laps.

For the 1952 season a lack of fully fledged F1 machinery bounced the FIA into running the world championship for F2 machines, effectively guaranteeing that the contest would be a private party for Alberto Ascari. Starting from second place on the grid, Ascari shot into the lead at the start and lapped the entire field. Mike Hawthorn's third in the Cooper-Bristol sowed the seeds of future optimism for spectating British fans.

1953, 18 July
SILVERSTONE, 90 laps of 2.927-mile circuit

1st, Alberto Ascari (Ferrari 500), 2h 50m, 92.98mph; 2nd, Juan Manuel Fangio (Maserati A6GCM), 2h 51m; 3rd, Giuseppe Farina (Ferrari 500), 88 laps; 4th, Froilan González (Maserati A6GCM), 88 laps; 5th, Mike Hawthorn (Ferrari 500), 87 laps; 6th, Felipe Bonetto (Maserati A6GCM), 82 laps.

For the second straight season the F2 regulations were used for the FIA world championship but this year Ascari had a little more on his plate in terms of firm opposition. With González delayed after his Maserati developed an oil leak and was black-flagged after ignoring pit signals to come in for a check-up, the race turned out to be a straight fight between Ascari and Fangio, although the Ferrari driver always had the upper hand and won by a minute.

1954, 17 July
SILVERSTONE, 90 laps of 2.927-mile circuit

1st, Froilan González (Ferrari 625), 2h 56m 14s, 89.69mph; 2nd, Mike Hawthorn (Ferrari 625), 2h 57m 24s; 3rd, Onofre Marimón (Maserati 250F), 89 laps; 4th, Juan Manuel Fangio (Mercedes-Benz W196), 89 laps; 5th, Maurice Trintignant (Ferrari 625), 87 laps; 6th, Roberto Mières (Maserati A6GCM), 87 laps.

Two weeks after the streamlined Mercedes-Benz W196s dominated the French Grand Prix at the super-fast Reims circuit, their drivers found Silverstone relatively tight and uncomfortable, with the result that the best Reims winner Fangio could manage was a lapped fourth. Instead, González, who had qualified second behind Fangio, led from start to finish to score his second British Grand Prix success at the Northamptonshire circuit.

1955, 16 July
AINTREE, 90 laps of 3-mile circuit

1st, Stirling Moss (Mercedes-Benz W196), 3h 7m 21.2s, 86.47mph; 2nd, Juan Manuel Fangio (Mercedes-Benz W196), 3h 7m 21.4s; 3rd, Karl Kling (Mercedes-Benz W196), 3h 8m 33.0s; 4th, Piero Taruffi (Mercedes-Benz W196), 89 laps; 5th, Luigi Musso (Maserati 250F), 89 laps; 6th, Mike Hawthorn/ Eugenio Castellotti (Ferrari 625), 87 laps.

Stirling Moss had been signed to drive for the works Mercedes team after impressing the legendary Alfred Neubauer with his ability behind the wheel of a private Maserati 250F the previous year. For much of the distance he diced with the legendary Fangio, scoring his first *grand épreuve* success by less than a length at the chequered flag. Mercedes finished in one-two-three-four formation.

1956, 14 July
SILVERSTONE, 101 laps of 2.927-mile circuit

1st, Juan Manuel Fangio (Lancia Ferrari D50), 2h 59m 47s, 98.66mph; 2nd, Marquis de Portago/Peter Collins (Lancia Ferrari D50), 100 laps; 3rd, Jean Behra (Maserati 250F), 99 laps; 4th, Jack Fairman (Connaught), 98 laps; 5th, Horace Gould (Maserati 250F), 97 laps; 6th, Luigi Villoresi (Maserati 250F), 96 laps.

There was much excitement at the start when the very quick BRM P25s of Mike Hawthorn and Tony Brooks raced away into the lead, but Hawthorn eventually stopped with a split grease seal in the car's transmission and Brooks ran off the road at Abbey after the throttle stuck, the former dental student being thrown out before the car erupted in flames. That left Fangio to score an easy win in one of the former Lancia D50s now reworked by the Maranello team.

1957, 20 July
AINTREE, 90 laps of 3-mile circuit

1st, Stirling Moss/Tony Brooks (Vanwall), 3h 6m 37.8s, 86.8mph; 2nd, Luigi Musso (Lancia Ferrari 801), 3h 7m 3.4s; 3rd, Mike Hawthorn (Lancia Ferrari 801), 3h 7m 20.6s; 4th, Maurice Trintignant/Peter Collins (Lancia Ferrari 801), 88 laps; 5th, Roy

Salvadori (Cooper-Climax T43), 85 laps; 6th, Bob Gerard (Cooper-Bristol T44), 82 laps.

Two years after achieving his Mercedes success at the Liverpool circuit, Stirling Moss battled to repeat the result at the wheel of the sleek British Vanwall. He built up a 22-second lead over Jean Behra's Maserati, but a misfire then twice forced him into the pits, after which he took over team-mate Brooks's car; Tony was still bruised and battered after an accident at Le Mans. Behra suffered an engine failure while leading, Mike Hawthorn's Ferrari punctured a tyre on the debris, and Moss nipped through to score a historic win.

1958, 19 July
SILVERSTONE, 75 laps of 2.927-mile circuit

1st, Peter Collins (Ferrari Dino 246), 2h 9m 4.2s, 102.05mph; 2nd, Mike Hawthorn (Ferrari Dino 246), 2h 9m 28.4s; 3rd, Roy Salvadori (Cooper-Climax T45), 2h 9m 54.8s; 4th, Stuart Lewis-Evans (Vanwall), 2h 9m 55.0s; 5th, Harry Schell (BRM P25), 2h 10m 19.0s; 6th, Jack Brabham (Cooper-Climax T45), 2h 10m 27.4s.

Although Stirling Moss grabbed pole position for Vanwall, this turned out to be a two-horse race for close friends and Ferrari team-mates Peter Collins and Mike Hawthorn, although Roy Salvadori's third-placed finish in the rear-engined Cooper-Climax hammered home the message writ large by Moss's victory in the Argentine Grand Prix at the start of the season. The days of the front-engined F1 car were indeed numbered.

1959, 18 July
AINTREE, 75 laps of 3-mile circuit

1st, Jack Brabham (Cooper-Climax T51), 2h 30m 11.6s, 89.88mph;

2nd, Stirling Moss (BRM P25), 2h 30m 33.8s; 3rd, Bruce McLaren (Cooper-Climax T51), 2h 30m 34.0s; 4th, Harry Schell (BRM P25), 74 laps; 5th, Maurice Trintignant (Cooper-Climax T51), 74 laps; 6th, Roy Salvadori (Aston Martin DBR4), 74 laps.

Brabham dominated this race in the works Cooper-Climax, leading from pole position and never seriously challenged for the entire distance. Stirling Moss, guesting in a BRP-prepared works BRM P25, managed to get to within ten seconds of him but eventually had to settle for second place after a late stop to top up with fuel. That allowed Brabham the luxury of being able to ease off and stroke his way home to the chequered flag.

1960, 16 July
SILVERSTONE, 77 laps of 2.927-mile circuit

1st, Jack Brabham (Cooper-Climax T53), 2h 4m 24.6s 108.69mph; 2nd, John Surtees (Lotus 18), 2h 5m 14.2s; 3rd, Innes Ireland (Lotus 18), 2h 5m 54.2s; 4th, Bruce McLaren (Cooper-Climax T53), 76 laps; 5th, Tony Brooks (Cooper-Climax T51), 76 laps; 6th, Wolfgang von Trips (Ferrari Dino 246), 74 laps.

This was a race made memorable by the fact that Graham Hill set the pace in the works BRM, leading until a few laps from the chequered flag only to spin off as he was lapping some slower cars under pressure from the wily Jack Brabham, who was then able to inherit another comfortable race victory. John Surtees performed sensationally on his grand prix debut to bring the works Lotus 18 home third ahead of the longer-established Innes Ireland.

1961, 15 July
AINTREE, 75 laps of 3-mile circuit

1st, Wolfgang von Trips (Ferrari 156), 2h 40m 53.6s, 83.91mph; 2nd, Phil Hill (Ferrari 156), 2h 41m 39.6s; 3rd, Richie Ginther (Ferrari 156), 2h 41m 40.4s; 4th, Jack Brabham (Cooper-Climax T55), 2h 42m 2.2s; 5th, Jo Bonnier (Porsche 718), 2h 42m 9.8s; 6th, Roy Salvadori (Cooper-Climax T53), 2h 42m 19.8s.

The 1961 season heralded the introduction of the new 1.5-litre regulations and Ferrari did the most convincing job with its new V6 power unit in the distinctive 'shark nose' challenger. The Aintree race took place in pouring rain and while pole man Phil Hill spun spectacularly in his Ferrari, Von Trips never put a wheel out of place in the treacherous conditions. Stirling Moss ran a strong second with the Rob Walker Lotus 18 before suffering brake problems and switching to the four-wheel-drive Ferguson P99.

1962, 21 July
AINTREE, 75 laps of 3-mile circuit

1st, Jim Clark (Lotus 25), 2h 26m 20.8s, 92.25mph; 2nd, John Surtees (Lola Mk4), 2h 27m 10.0s; 3rd, Bruce McLaren (Cooper-Climax T60), 2h 28m 5.6s; 4th, Graham Hill (BRM P57), 2h 28m 17.6s; 5th, Jack Brabham (Lotus 24), 74 laps; 6th, Tony Maggs (Cooper-Climax T60), 74 laps.

This race marked the start of a new F1 era for British fans, with the first outing on home soil for the seminal monocoque Lotus 25 in the hands of the matchless Jim Clark. He was fastest in practice by half a second and simply ran away with the race unchallenged to win comfortably from John Surtees in the Bowmaker Lola. It would the first of four straight victories in the British Grand Prix for the Scot.

1963, 20 July
SILVERSTONE, 82 laps of 2.927-mile circuit

1st, Jim Clark (Lotus 25), 2h 14m 9.6s, 107.34mph; 2nd, John Surtees (Ferrari 156), 2h 14m 35.4s; 3rd, Graham Hill (BRM P57), 2h 14m 47.2s; 4th, Richie Ginther (BRM P57), 81 laps; 5th, Lorenzo Bandini (BRM P57), 81 laps; 6th, Jim Hall (Lotus 24), 80 laps.

Clark qualified on pole position, as was becoming his habit, but he was slow off the line on this rare occasion, allowing the Brabhams of Jack and Dan Gurney to complete the opening lap in one-two formation. But by lap four Jimmy had claimed his regular position at the front of the field and built up a lead of almost a minute before easing off in the closing stages. Graham Hill looked on course for second place, but his BRM spluttered low on fuel at Stowe on the last lap, allowing Surtees through in his Ferrari.

1964, 11 July
BRANDS HATCH, 80 laps of 2.65-mile circuit

1st, Jim Clark (Lotus 25B), 2h 15m 7.0s, 94.14mph; 2nd, Graham Hill (BRM P261), 2h 15m 9.8s; 3rd, John Surtees (Ferrari 158), 2h 16m 27.6s; 4th, Jack Brabham (Brabham BT7), 79 laps; 5th, Lorenzo Bandini (Ferrari 156), 78 laps; 6th, Phil Hill (Cooper-Climax T73), 78 laps.

This was the first visit by the F1 championship brigade to Brands Hatch, kicking off a process of alternating the fixture with Silverstone that would last for more than two decades until after the 1986 event. Clark preferred to race the 'interim' Lotus 25B rather than the new type 33, but it made no difference to the outcome of the race. He led all the way and, although

Hill closed up a little over the last couple of laps, Clark had everything under control in his usual masterly fashion.

1965, 10 July
SILVERSTONE, 80 laps of 2.927-mile circuit

1st, Jim Clark (Lotus 33), 2h 5m 25.4s, 112.02mph; 2nd, Graham Hill (BRM P261), 2h 5m 28.6s; 3rd, John Surtees (Ferrari 1512), 2h 5m 53.0s; 4th, Mike Spence (Lotus 33), 2h 6m 5.0s; 5th, Jackie Stewart (BRM P261), 2h 6m 40.0s; 6th, Dan Gurney (Brabham BT11), 79 laps.

The final British Grand Prix to take place under the 1.5-litre regulations was noteworthy for the participation of the very powerful Honda in the hands of Richie Ginther, the American qualifying the Japanese machine on the front row of the grid and leading the race as far as Stowe corner on the opening lap. From then it was Jimmy Clark all the way, his Lotus slowed only in the closing stages by low oil pressure, but he nursed the car sympathetically home for another win ahead of Graham Hill's BRM.

1966, 16 July
BRANDS HATCH, 80 laps of 2.65-mile circuit

1st, Jack Brabham (Brabham-Repco BT19), 2h 13m 13.4s, 95.48mph; 2nd, Denny Hulme (Brabham-Repco BT20), 2h 13m 23s; 3rd, Graham Hill (BRM P261), 79 laps; 4th, Jim Clark (Lotus 33), 79 laps; 5th, Jochen Rindt (Cooper-Maserati T81), 79 laps; 6th, Bruce McLaren (McLaren-Serenissima M2B), 78 laps.

In the first season of the new 3-litre F1, Jack Brabham's agile machines powered by the lightweight Australian-built Repco

V8s proved both versatile and effective. The 44-year-old from Sydney demonstrated this with a comfortable win at Brands Hatch on his way to his third world championship title. His dogged team-mate Denny Hulme followed him home and the rest of the pack was more than a lap adrift.

1967, 15 July
SILVERSTONE, 80 laps of 2.927-mile circuit

1st, Jim Clark (Lotus 49), 1h 59m 25.6s, 117.64mph; 2nd, Denny Hulme (Brabham-Repco BT24), 1h 59m 38.4s; 3rd, Chris Amon (Ferrari 312), 1h 59m 42.2s; 4th, Jack Brabham (Brabham-Repco BT24), 1h 59m 47.4s; 5th, Pedro Rodriguez (Cooper-Maserati T81), 79 laps; 6th, John Surtees (Honda RA273), 78 laps.

This race proved to be a tour de force for the all-new Lotus 49s driven by Graham Hill and Jim Clark, the Londoner leading initially before pitting to have a loose rear-suspension bolt replaced and then retiring for good with an engine failure. That left Jimmy able to cruise home to his fifth British Grand Prix win in six years ahead of Hulme's Brabham, while Chris Amon just managed to out-fox Jack himself to surge through into third place shortly before the finish.

1968, 20 July
BRANDS HATCH, 80 laps of 2.65-mile circuit

1st, Jo Siffert (Lotus 49B), 2h 1m 20.3s, 104.83mph; 2nd, Chris Amon (Ferrari 312), 2h 1m 24.7s; 3rd, Jacky Ickx (Ferrari 312), 79 laps; 4th, Denny Hulme (McLaren M7A), 79 laps; 5th, John Surtees (Honda RA301), 78 laps; 6th, Jackie Stewart (Matra MS10), 78 laps.

The Lotus factory battled against the odds to have Rob

Walker's brand-new Lotus 49B ready for Jo Siffert to drive in this race and this dogged determination was rewarded by the Swiss driver picking up Team Lotus's fallen standard after the works cars of Graham Hill and Jackie Oliver suffered mechanical failures. Siffert was under pressure from Chris Amon's Ferrari all the way, but apart from a brief spell ahead of the blue-liveried Lotus had no answer for the Swiss driver in the closing stages.

1969, 19 July
SILVERSTONE, 84 laps of 2.927-mile circuit

1st, Jackie Stewart (Matra MS80), 1h 55m 55.6s, 127.25mph; 2nd, Jacky Ickx (Brabham BT26), 83 laps; 3rd, Bruce McLaren (McLaren M7C), 83 laps; 4th, Jochen Rindt (Lotus 49B), 83 laps; 5th, Piers Courage (Brabham BT26A), 83 laps; 6th, Vic Elford (McLaren M7A), 82 laps.

This was one of the most sensational of all the races dealt with between these covers. Stewart and Jochen Rindt were regarded as the two best drivers of their era, and were close friends, and this race went into the history books as one of their most epic confrontations. Stewart's Tyrrell Matra and Rindt's works Lotus went at it hammer and tongs from the start, swapping the lead all around the circuit. Eventually Rindt had to pit with a loose rear-wing end-plate. He subsequently stopped a second time to top up with fuel, allowing Stewart an unchallenged victory.

1970, 18 July
BRANDS HATCH, 80 laps of 2.65-mile circuit

1st, Jochen Rindt (Lotus 72C), 1h 57m 2.0s, 108.69mph;

2nd, Jack Brabham (Brabham BT33), 1h 57m 34.9s; 3rd, Denny Hulme (McLaren M14D), 1h 57m 56.4s; 4th, Clay Regazzoni (Ferrari 312B), 1h 57m 56.8s; 5th, Chris Amon (March 701), 79 laps; 6th, Graham Hill (Lotus 49C), 79 laps.

Jack Brabham looked in absolute control of this race from the start, but fuel pick-up problems caused by a mechanic adjusting the mixture to full rich before he took up his place on the grid meant that his tanks ran low on the last lap and Rindt pipped him at the post.

1971, 17 July
SILVERSTONE, 68 laps of 2.927-mile circuit

1st, Jackie Stewart (Tyrrell 003), 1h 31m 31.5s, 130.48mph; 2nd, Ronnie Peterson (March 711), 1h 32m 7.6s; 3rd, Emerson Fittipaldi (Lotus 72D), 1h 32m 22.0s; 4th, Henri Pescarolo (March 711), 67 laps; 5th, Rolf Stommelen (Surtees TS9), 67 laps; 6th, John Surtees (Surtees TS9), 67 laps.

Two years after winning at Silverstone for Matra, Jackie Stewart was now at the wheel of the similarly competitive Tyrrell 003 and well on the way to the second of his three world championships. Stewart stamped his mastery on the event, out-distancing Ronnie Peterson's March 711 by more than half a minute. Emerson Fittipaldi, the man who replaced Rindt in the Lotus line-up after his death, finished third.

1972, 15 July
BRANDS HATCH, 76 laps of 2.65-mile circuit

1st, Emerson Fittipaldi (Lotus 72D), 1h 47m 50.2s, 112.06mph; 2nd, Jackie Stewart (Tyrrell 003), 1h 47m 54.3s; 3rd, Peter Revson (McLaren M19A), 1h 49m 2.7s; 4th, Chris Amon (Matra

MS120C), 75 laps; 5th, Denny Hulme (McLaren M19C), 75 laps; 6th, Arturo Merzario (Ferrari 312B2), 75 laps.

Jacky Ickx led the opening stages before his Ferrari B2 wilted and Emerson Fittipaldi, now very much into the swing of things with the further-developed Lotus 72, moved ahead. Over the bumps and undulations of the Kent circuit the Lotus seemed to be giving its Brazilian driver an easier ride than Jackie Stewart's pursuing Tyrrell and although the reigning world champion hung on gamely he was 4.1 seconds adrift at the chequered flag.

1973, 14 July
SILVERSTONE, 67 laps of 2.927-mile circuit

1st, Peter Revson (McLaren M23), 1h 29m 18.5s, 131.75mph; 2nd, Ronnie Peterson (Lotus 72E), 1h 29m 21.3s; 3rd, Denny Hulme (McLaren M23), 1h 29m 21.5s; 4th, James Hunt (March 731), 1h 29m 21.9s; 5th, François Cevert (Tyrrell 006), 1h 29m 55.1s; 6th, Carlos Reutemann (Brabham BT42), 1h 30m 3.2s.

This was the race that exploded into the history books, almost literally, when Jody Scheckter spun his McLaren coming out of Woodcote on the opening lap, triggering a multi-car pile-up that wrecked half the field and caused the race to be red-flagged to a halt. After Andrea de Adamich was cut out of his wrecked Brabham the race was restarted and Peter Revson held on well at the head of the queue to win by just under a couple of seconds.

1974, 20 July
BRANDS HATCH, 75 laps of 2.65-mile circuit

1st, Jody Scheckter (Tyrrell 007), 1h 43m 2.2s, 115.74mph; 2nd, Emerson Fittipaldi (McLaren M23), 1h 43m 17.5s; 3rd, Jacky Ickx (Lotus 72E), 1h 44m 3.7s; 4th, Clay Regazzoni (Ferrari

312B3), 1h 44m 9.4s; 5th, Niki Lauda (Ferrari 312B3), 74 laps; 6th, Carlos Reutemann (Brabham BT44), 74 laps.

This was a race Niki Lauda seemed to have in his pocket from the word go until he picked up a slow puncture in his Ferrari's right-rear tyre as he got into the closing stages. He elected to stay out even though he had been overtaken by the eventual winner Jody Scheckter, but then pitted for replacement rubber shortly before the finish. Amazingly, the pit lane was blocked and he was unable to resume, but was awarded fifth after an inquiry by the FIA.

1975, 19 July
SILVERSTONE, 56 laps of 2.932-mile circuit
1st, Emerson Fittipaldi (McLaren M23), 1h 22m 5.0s, 120.02mph; 2nd, Carlos Pace (Brabham BT44B), not running; 3rd, Jody Scheckter (Tyrrell 007), not running; 4th, James Hunt (Hesketh 308), not running; 5th, Mark Donohue (March 751), not running; 6th, Vittorio Brambilla (March 751), not running.

A torrential downpour resulted in this race being red-flagged with 12 racing laps still to go, allowing Emerson Fittipaldi to luck into the final victory of his F1 career as most of the other competitors' cars lay scattered in catch-fencing and run-off areas all around the circuit. Tom Pryce had qualified the Shadow DN5 brilliantly on pole position and was challenging in the leading bunch when he too was caught out by a damp patch and skidded off at Becketts.

1976, 18 July
BRANDS HATCH, 76 laps of 2.614-mile circuit
1st (disqualified) James Hunt (McLaren M23), 1h 43m 27.61s,

115.21mph; 2nd, Niki Lauda (Ferrari 312T2), 1h 44m 19.66s; 3rd, Jody Scheckter (Tyrrell P34), 1h 44m 35.84s; 4th, John Watson (Penske PC4), 75 laps; 5th, Tom Pryce (Shadow DN5B), 75 laps; 6th, Alan Jones (Surtees TS19), 75 laps.

Another controversial British Grand Prix, with the race being red-flagged at the end of the opening lap. James Hunt, who at that point was not running, was still permitted to take the restart by the stewards, although he was to be stripped of his subsequent convincing win by the FIA, which handed the victory to his arch rival Niki Lauda.

1977, 16 July
SILVERSTONE, 68 laps of 2.932-mile circuit
1st, James Hunt (McLaren M26), 1h 31m 46.06s, 130.36mph; 2nd, Niki Lauda (Ferrari 312T2), 1h 32m 4.37s; 3rd, Gunnar Nilsson (Lotus 78), 1h 32m 5.63s; 4th, Jochen Mass (McLaren M26), 1h 32m 33.82s; 5th, Hans-Joachim Stuck (Brabham BT45B), 1h 32m 57.79s; 6th, Jacques Laffite (Ligier JS7), 67 laps.

This was a race in which John Watson had the legs of his rivals in the opening stages at the wheel of Bernie Ecclestone's Alfa flat-12-engined Brabham BT45. Unfortunately his fine performance was ruined by a fuel pick-up problem, allowing Hunt to score a strong win over a brake-troubled Lauda's Ferrari.

1978, 16 July
BRANDS HATCH, 76 laps of 2.614-mile circuit
1st, Carlos Reutemann (Ferrari 312T3), 1h 42m 12.39s, 116.63mph; 2nd, Niki Lauda (Brabham BT46), 1h 42m 13.62s; 3rd, John Watson (Brabham BT46), 1h 42m 49.64s; 4th, Patrick Depailler

(Tyrrell 008), 1h 43m 25.66s; 5th, Hans-Joachim Stuck (Shadow DN9), 75 laps; 6th, Patrick Tambay (McLaren M26), 75 laps.

From the start the race was dominated by the superbly impressive ground-effect Lotus 79s driven by Mario Andretti and Ronnie Peterson in tight formation at the head of the field, but both suffered engine failures. Their retirements left Niki Lauda's Brabham leading from Carlos Reutemann's Ferrari, but Niki was momentarily blocked lapping Bruno Giacomelli's McLaren M26 at Clearways and Carlos nipped through the gap.

1979, 14 July
SILVERSTONE, 68 laps of 2.932-mile circuit

1st, Clay Regazzoni (Williams FW07), 1h 26m 11.17s, 138.80mph; 2nd, René Arnoux (Renault RS10), 1h 26m 35.45s; 3rd, Jean-Pierre Jarier (Tyrrell 009), 67 laps; 4th, John Watson (McLaren M29), 67 laps; 5th, Jody Scheckter (Ferrari 312T4), 67 laps; 6th, Jacky Ickx (Ligier JS11), 67 laps.

Only a cracked water pump casting prevented a dominant Alan Jones from scoring the first grand prix victory for Frank Williams's team, but his number two, Clay Regazzoni, filled the supporting role and was ready to scoop the laurels in fine style. Behind Arnoux and Jarier, John Watson gave the new McLaren M29 a promising debut, squeezing past Scheckter's Ferrari on the final lap.

1980, 13 July
BRANDS HATCH, 76 laps of 2.614-mile circuit

1st, Alan Jones (Williams FW07B), 1h 34m 49.228s, 125.71mph; 2nd, Nelson Piquet (Brabham BT49), 1h 35m 0.235s; 3rd, Carlos Reutemann (Williams FW07B), 1h 35m 2.513s; 4th Derek Daly

(Tyrrell 010), 75 laps; 5th, Jean-Pierre Jarier (Tyrrell 010), 75 laps; 6th, Alain Prost (McLaren M29), 75 laps.

The Ligiers of Didier Pironi and Jacques Laffite were very much the pace-setters during qualifying, buttoning up the front row of the starting grid. But after they both hit trouble Jones won commandingly from Nelson Piquet's Brabham and the new Williams number two, Carlos Reutemann, who had a steady run to third. Reutemann, who'd accepted number-two status to switch from Lotus, was just happy to be in a competitive car.

1981, 18 July
SILVERSTONE, 68 laps of 2.932-mile circuit
1st, John Watson (McLaren MP4), 1h 26m 54.80s, 137.64mph; 2nd, Carlos Reutemann (Williams FW07C), 1h 27m 35.45s; 3rd, Jacques Laffite (Ligier JS11), 67 laps; 4th, Eddie Cheever (Tyrrell 010), 67 laps; 5th, Hector Rebaque (Brabham BT49C), 67 laps; 6th, Slim Borgudd (ATS HGS1), 67 laps.

Although the Renault turbos of René Arnoux and Alain Prost buttoned up the front row of the starting grid, Prost was an early retirement and Watson, driving the ground-breaking carbon-fibre composite McLaren MP4, gradually hauled in Arnoux's misfiring machine to score a historic victory while Arnoux dropped down the field. Reutemann, now comfortably leading the title chase, bet me £25 that he would not eventually take the championship. And he was right!

1982, 18 July
BRANDS HATCH, 76 laps of 2.614-mile circuit
1st, Niki Lauda (McLaren MP4B), 1h 35m 33.812s, 124.73mph;

2nd, Didier Pironi (Ferrari 126C2), 1h 35m 59.538s; 3rd, Patrick Tambay (Ferrari 126C2), 1h 36m 12.248s; 4th, Elio de Angelis (Lotus 91), 1h 36m 15.054s; 5th, Derek Daly (Williams FW08), 1h 36m 15.242s; 6th, Alain Prost (Renault RE30B), 1h 36m 15.448s.

This was the race at which the Brabham-BMW team reintroduced in-race, high-pressure refuelling, calculating that Nelson Piquet's BT50 would be able to build up enough of a lead on light tanks before stopping to top up. In the event, Piquet retired early on and it was left to Brands Hatch favourite Niki Lauda to score a popular win for McLaren.

1983, 16 July
SILVERSTONE, 67 laps of 2.932-mile circuit

1st, Alain Prost (Renault RE40), 1h 24m 39.78s, 139.22mph; 2nd, Nelson Piquet (Brabham BT52B), 1h 24m 58.941s; 3rd, Patrick Tambay (Ferrari 126C3), 1h 25m 6.026s; 4th, Nigel Mansell (Lotus 94T), 1h 25m 18.732s; 5th, René Arnoux (Ferrari 126C3), 1h 25m 38.654s; 6th, Niki Lauda (McLaren MP4/1C), 66 laps.

In airless and unusually torrid conditions, Prost's Renault won easily after an early challenge from the two Ferraris had faded. Meanwhile, Nigel Mansell proved to be the star of the show in the recently completed Renault turbo-engined Lotus 94T, which flew through the field to fourth after being completed only on the morning of first practice.

1983 (European Grand Prix), 25 September
BRANDS HATCH, 76 laps of 2.614-mile circuit

1st, Nelson Piquet (Brabham BT52B), 1h 36m 45.865s, 123.184mph; 2nd, Alain Prost (Renault RE40), 1h 36m 52.436s; 3rd, Nigel Mansell (Lotus 94T), 1h 37m 16.18s; 4th, Andrea de

Cesaris (Alfa Romeo 183T), 1h 37m 20.261s; 5th, Derek Warwick (Toleman TG183B), 1h 37m 30.780s; 6th, Bruno Giacomelli (Toleman TG183B), 1h 37m 38.055s.

Brands Hatch may have faced losing its deal to alternate the British Grand Prix with Silverstone after 1986, but in the early 1980s it was felt there was enough interest for the UK to stage a second round of the world championship, with two at Brands Hatch (1983 and 1985) plus the memorable event at Donington Park (1993). This race was won easily by world champion-elect Nelson Piquet's Brabham.

1984, 22 July
BRANDS HATCH, 71 laps of 2.614-mile circuit
1st, Niki Lauda (McLaren MP4/2), 1h 29m 28.532s, 124.46mph; 2nd, Derek Warwick (Renault RE50), 1h 30m 10.655s; 3rd, Ayrton Senna (Toleman TG184), 1h 30m 31.86s; 4th, Elio de Angelis (Lotus 95T), 70 laps; 5th, Michele Alboreto (Ferrari 126C4), 70 laps; 6th, René Arnoux (Ferrari 126C4), 70 laps.

Nelson Piquet led for the first 11 laps in his Brabham-BMW, before Alain Prost went ahead and seemed on course for victory in his McLaren-TAG. Unfortunately the Frenchman's machine succumbed to a gearbox pinion failure, allowing his team-mate Niki Lauda through to take his second win in three years at the circuit.

1985, 21 July
SILVERSTONE, 65 laps of 2.932-mile circuit
1st, Alain Prost (McLaren MP4/2B), 1h 18m 10.436s, 146.27mph; 2nd, Michele Alboreto (Ferrari 156/85), 64 laps; 3rd, Jacques Laffite (Ligier JS25), 64 laps; 4th, Nelson Piquet (Brabham

209

BT54), 63 laps; 5th, Derek Warwick (Renault RE60B), 64 laps; 6th, Marc Surer (Brabham BT54), 63 laps.

Keke Rosberg stormed to pole in the Williams-Honda FW10 at an average speed just topping the 160mph mark, but a broken exhaust sidelined him in the race. Ayrton Senna's Lotus was the star of the show, leading the opening stages until its fuel injection system went awry. That allowed Prost through to an easy victory one lap ahead of Alboreto.

1985 (European Grand Prix), 6 October
BRANDS HATCH, 75 laps of 2.614-mile circuit
1st, Nigel Mansell (Williams FW10), 1h 32m 58.109s, 126.527mph; 2nd, Ayrton Senna (Lotus 97T), 1h 33m 19.505s; 3rd, Keke Rosberg (Williams FW10), 1h 33m 56.642s; 4th, Alain Prost (McLaren MP4/2B), 1h 34m 4.23s; 5th, Elio de Angelis (Lotus 97T), 74 laps; 6th, Thierry Boutsen (Arrows A8), 73 laps.

This was Mansell's great day, which he had confidently predicted would come about five years earlier when he made his F1 debut driving a Lotus in the Austrian Grand Prix. Senna's Lotus led the opening stages and, after Nelson Piquet's Brabham tangled with Rosberg's Williams, Nigel had a clear run to the chequered flag in front of his delighted fans.

1986, 13 July
BRANDS HATCH, 75 laps of 2.61-mile circuit
1st, Nigel Mansell (Williams FW11), 1h 30m 38.471s, 129.78mph; 2nd, Nelson Piquet (Williams FW11), 1h 30m 44.045s; 3rd, Alain Prost (McLaren MP4/2C), 74 laps; 4th, René Arnoux (Ligier JS27), 73 laps; 5th, Martin Brundle (Tyrrell 015), 72 laps; 6th, Philippe Streiff (Tyrrell 015), 72 laps.

The Williams-Honda FW11 turbos were in an absolute class of their own, although the race was stopped and restarted after a terrible first-corner accident that left Ligier driver Jacques Laffite hospitalised with serious leg injuries after crashing at Paddock. Piquet stormed ahead at the restart, but when he missed a gear on lap 23 Mansell was through and never again challenged.

1987, 12 July
SILVERSTONE, 65 laps of 2.969-mile circuit
1st, Nigel Mansell (Williams FW11B), 1h 19m 11.78s, 146.208mph; 2nd, Nelson Piquet (Williams FW11B), 1h 19m 13.698s; 3rd, Ayrton Senna (Lotus 99T), 64 laps; 4th, Satoru Nakajima (Lotus 99T), 63 laps; 5th, Derek Warwick (Arrows A10), 63 laps; 6th, Teo Fabi (Benetton B187), 63 laps.

Another all-Williams battle between intense rivals Piquet and Mansell, with the Brazilian leading the early stages of the race. Mansell initially kept pace but became increasingly worried by a front-wheel vibration caused by a lost balance weight. He stopped at the end of lap 35 for fresh tyres, resuming 28 seconds behind the Brazilian and against the odds hauled him in and double-bluffed him out of the lead with a brilliant manoeuvre at 180mph going into Stowe on the penultimate lap.

1988, 10 July
SILVERSTONE, 65 laps of 2.969-mile circuit
1st, Ayrton Senna (McLaren MP4/4), 1h 33m 16.367s, 124.14mph; 2nd, Nigel Mansell (Williams FW12), 1h 33m 39.711s; 3rd, Alessandro Nannini (Benetton B188), 1h 34m

7.581s; 4th, Mauricio Gugelmin (March 881), 1h 34m 27.745s; 5th, Nelson Piquet (Lotus 100T), 1h 34m 37.202s; 6th, Derek Warwick (Arrows A10B), 64 laps.

Gerhard Berger's Ferrari led for the first 13 of these saturated laps before Ayrton Senna's McLaren-Honda turbo-surged through to lead all the way to the chequered flag. Nigel Mansell was again star of the show, this time in the 3.5-litre Judd-engined Williams, climbing through to second place after the car had been re-engineered without its active-ride suspension in the run-up to the race.

1989, 16 July
SILVERSTONE, 64 laps of 2.97-mile circuit
1st, Alain Prost (McLaren MP4/5), 1h 19m 22.131s, 143.69mph; 2nd, Nigel Mansell (Ferrari 640), 1h 19m 41.5s; 3rd, Alessandro Nannini (Benetton B189), 1h 20m 10.15s; 4th, Nelson Piquet (Lotus 101), 1h 20m 28.866s; 5th, Pierluigi Martini (Minardi M189), 63 laps; 6th, Luis Sala (Minardi M189), 63 laps.

Ayrton Senna led from the start in the new V10-engined McLaren-Honda, but it was soon clear he was battling a gear-change glitch, which ended with him spinning to a halt in a track-side gravel trap. Thereafter Prost had a relatively easy run to victory, although Mansell, now driving for Ferrari, kept him on his toes and set the fastest race lap in the process.

1990, 15 July
SILVERSTONE, 64 laps of 2.97-mile circuit
1st, Alain Prost (Ferrari 641/2), 1h 18m 30.999s, 145.25mph; 2nd, Thierry Boutsen (Williams FW13B), 1h 19m 10.091s; 3rd, Ayrton Senna (McLaren MP4/5B), 1h 19m 14.087s; 4th, Eric

Bernard (Lola 90), 1h 19m 46.30s; 5th, Nelson Piquet (Benetton B190), 1h 19m 55.002s; 6th, Aguri Suzuki (Lola 90), 63 laps.

Senna's McLaren led the opening phase, but Mansell was pumped up to give Prost a driving lesson on his home turf and soon surged through to take the lead. But Nigel's hopes of a fourth F1 victory in front of his home crowd were thwarted when his Ferrari's semi-automatic transmission packed up and he was out, leaving the Frenchman in complete control.

1991, 14 July
SILVERSTONE, 59 laps of 3.247-mile circuit
1st, Nigel Mansell (Williams FW14), 1h 27m 35.479s; 2nd, Gerhard Berger (McLaren MP4/6), 1h 28m 17.722s; 3rd, Alain Prost (Ferrari 643), 1h 28m 35.629s; 4th, Ayrton Senna (McLaren MP4/6), 58 laps; 5th, Nelson Piquet (Benetton B191), 58 laps; 6th, Bertrand Gachot (Jordan 191), 58 laps.

This was Mansell at his explosive best in the superb Williams FW14. He started from pole and led every inch of the way, the latest Williams completely out-running the much-fancied opposition from Ferrari and McLaren. Ayrton Senna actually ran out of fuel in his McLaren thanks to the thirst of the latest Honda V12 engine.

1992, 12 July
SILVERSTONE, 59 laps of 3.247-mile circuit
1st, Nigel Mansell (Williams FW14B), 1h 25m 42.991s, 134.11mph; 2nd, Riccardo Patrese (Williams FW14B), 1h 26m 22.085s; 3rd, Martin Brundle (Benetton B192), 1h 26m 31.386s; 4th, Michael Schumacher (Benetton B192), 1h 26m 36.258s;

5th, Gerhard Berger (McLaren MP4/7A), 1h 26m 38.786s; 6th, Mika Häkkinen (Lotus 107), 1h 27m 3.129s.

This was almost a copy-book re-run of the previous year's race, but this time with Riccardo Patrese rounding off a seamless Williams one-two. Martin Brundle drove a fabulous race in the Benetton to see off new star Michael Schumacher for the final place on the podium and a young Finn named Mika Häkkinen came home sixth for Lotus. Much more would be heard of him very soon.

1993 (European Grand Prix), 11 April
DONINGTON PARK, 76 laps of 2.5-mile circuit

1st, Ayrton Senna (McLaren MP4/8), 1h 50m 46.57s, 102.901mph; 2nd, Damon Hill (Williams FW15C), 1h 52m 9.769s; 3rd, Alain Prost (Williams FW15C), 75 laps; 4th, Johnny Herbert (Lotus 107B), 75 laps; 5th, Riccardo Patrese (Benetton B193B), 74 laps; 6th, Fabrizio Barbazza (Minardi M193), 74 laps.

One of the classic F1 races of all time and one of the cornerstones for the very existence of this book. Tom Wheatcroft always wanted such a race. Bernie Ecclestone and Ayrton Senna delivered just exactly what was needed to rekindle the passion generated by the two pre-war Donington Grands Prix. But it was a one-off, not a trailer for things to come.

1993, 11 July
SILVERSTONE, 59 laps of 3.247-mile circuit

1st, Alain Prost (Williams FW15C), 1h 25m 38.189s, 134.24mph; 2nd, Michael Schumacher (Benetton B193B), 1h 25m 45.849s; 3rd, Riccardo Patrese (Benetton B193B), 1h 26m 55.671s; 4th, Johnny Herbert (Lotus 107B), 1h 26m 56.596s; 5th, Ayrton Senna (McLaren

MP4/8), 58 laps; 6th, Derek Warwick (Footwork FA14), 58 laps.

It seemed as though Damon Hill might be about to take over where Nigel Mansell left off by delivering the big result for the patriotic crowd. But, although Damon led for the first 41 laps, he was eventually sidelined by a spectacular Renault engine failure and had to sit and watch as Prost surged home for the win.

1994, 10 July
SILVERSTONE, 60 laps of 3.142-mile circuit
1st, Damon Hill (Williams FW16), 1h 30m 3.64s, 125.61mph; 2nd (disqualified) Michael Schumacher (Benetton B194), 1h 30m 22.418s; 3rd, Jean Alesi (Ferrari 412T1B), 1h 31m 11.768s; 4th, Mika Häkkinen (McLaren MP4/9), 1h 31m 44.299s; 5th, Rubens Barrichello (Jordan 194), 1h 31m 45.391s; 6th, David Coulthard (Williams FW16), 59 laps.

Damon Hill chased Michael Schumacher hard in the opening stages, but Schumacher had breached the rules by overtaking on the parade lap and later ignoring the black flag for several laps, understandably ending up disqualified. That left Damon a clear run to victory, receiving his trophy from star guest the Princess of Wales, who joined him on the rostrum.

1995, 16 July
SILVERSTONE, 61 laps of 3.142-mile circuit
1st, Johnny Herbert (Benetton B195), 1h 34m 35.093s, 121.59mph; 2nd, Jean Alesi (Ferrari 412T2), 1h 34m 51.572s; 3rd, David Coulthard (Williams FW17), 1h 34m 58.981s; 4th, Olivier Panis (Ligier JS41), 1h 36m 8.261s; 5th, Mark Blundell (McLaren MP4/10B), 1h 36m 23.265s; 6th, Heinz-Harald Frentzen (Sauber C14), 60 laps.

Again it was Hill against Schumacher for the win, with Michael anxious to make up for what he felt was the humiliation of the previous year and Damon wanting to get even for being turfed off the road in Adelaide the previous autumn. The two collided spectacularly, gifting Herbert the first of his three career F1 victories.

1996, 14 July
SILVERSTONE, 61 laps of 3.152-mile circuit

1st, Jacques Villeneuve (Williams FW18), 1h 33m 0.874s, 124.01mph; 2nd, Gerhard Berger (Benetton B196), 1h 33m 19.9s; 3rd, Mika Häkkinen (McLaren MP4/11B), 1h 33m 51.704s; 4th, Rubens Barrichello (Jordan 196), 1h 34m 7.59s; 5th, David Coulthard (McLaren MP4/11B), 1h 34m 23.381s; 6th, Martin Brundle (Jordan 196), 60 laps.

Damon Hill's hopes of a second British Grand Prix victory were thwarted by a loose front wheel nut, which pitched him into a spectacular spin on the approach to Copse. His team-mate Jacques Villeneuve had pretty much dominated the race from the start, apart from a six-lap stint during which Jean Alesi popped ahead in his Benetton, but Alesi later retired.

1997, 13 July
SILVERSTONE, 59 laps of 3.194-mile circuit

1st, Jacques Villeneuve (Williams FW19), 1h 28m 1.665s, 128.44mph; 2nd, Jean Alesi (Benetton B197), 1h 28m 11.87s; 3rd, Alex Wurz (Benetton B197), 1h 28m 12.961s; 4th, David Coulthard (McLaren MP4/12), 1h 28m 32.894s; 5th, Ralf Schumacher (Jordan 197), 1h 28m 33.545s; 6th, Damon Hill (Arrows A18), 1h 29m 15.217s.

Villeneuve came back for more in 1998, winning from a Benetton two-three by Alesi and Alex Wurz, although Mika Häkkinen's McLaren-Merc had seemed to be romping away to the Finn's maiden victory when its engine failed with only seven laps to go. Damon Hill was sixth in his Arrows-Yamaha, a dramatic contrast to his previous pace with Williams.

1998, 12 July
SILVERSTONE, 60 laps of 3.194-mile circuit
1st, Michael Schumacher (Ferrari F300), 1h 47m 2.450s, 107.38mph; 2nd, Mika Häkkinen (McLaren MP4/13), 1h 47m 24.915s; 3rd, Eddie Irvine (Ferrari F300), 1h 47m 31.649s; 4th, Alex Wurz (Benetton B198), 59 laps; 5th, Giancarlo Fisichella (Benetton B198), 59 laps; 6th, Ralf Schumacher (Jordan 198), 59 laps.

A curious race indeed. Schumacher was called into the pits to serve a penalty for overtaking behind the safety car, but was able to delay it until the final lap and instead was given a ten-second penalty, which was withdrawn subsequently because it had been imposed incorrectly. Häkkinen s McLaren ran well to second ahead of Irvine in the other Ferrari.

1999, 11 July
SILVERSTONE, 60 laps of 3.194-mile circuit
1st, David Coulthard (McLaren MP4/14), 1h 32m 30.144s, 124.26mph; 2nd, Eddie Irvine (Ferrari F399), 1h 32m 31.973s; 3rd, Ralf Schumacher (Williams FW21), 1h 32m 57.555s; 4th, Heinz-Harald Frentzen (Jordan 199), 1h 32m 57.933s; 5th, Damon Hill (Jordan 199), 1h 33m 8.75s; 6th, Pedro Diniz (Sauber C18), 1h 33m 23.787s.

The race was stopped at the end of the opening lap after Michael Schumacher fractured a leg when he slammed his Ferrari hard into the tyre wall. Once it got going again, Häkkinen retired after leading the first 24 laps, then Irvine went ahead but slightly over-shot his refuelling rig at the final round of stops. That delay allowed Coulthard to get by.

2000, 23 April
SILVERSTONE, 60 laps of 3.194-mile circuit

1st, David Coulthard (McLaren MP4/15), 1h 28m 50.108s, 129.41mph; 2nd, Mika Häkkinen (McLaren MP4/15), 1h 28m 51.585s; 3rd, Michael Schumacher (Ferrari F1 2000), 1h 29m 10.025s; 4th, Ralf Schumacher (Williams FW22), 1h 29m 31.42s; 5th, Jenson Button (Williams FW22), 1h 29m 47.867s; 6th, Jarno Trulli (Jordan EJ10), 1h 30m 9.381s.

Silverstone was allocated what turned out to be a most uncomfortable Easter weekend fixture and a rainy winter ensured that the car parks were glutinous mud baths. The race was led by new Ferrari recruit Rubens Barrichello in the opening stages, but then it turned into a McLaren-fest with Coulthard winning again, this time ahead of team-mate Häkkinen.

2001, 15 July
SILVERSTONE, 60 laps of 3.194-mile circuit

1st, Mika Häkkinen (McLaren MP4/16), 1h 25m 33.77s, 134.36mph; 2nd, Michael Schumacher (Ferrari F2001), 1h 26m 7.416s; 3rd, Rubens Barrichello (Ferrari F2001), 1h 26m 33.051s; 4th, Juan Pablo Montoya (Williams FW23), 1h 26m 42.542s; 5th, Kimi Räikkönen (Sauber C20), 59 laps; 6th, Nick Heidfeld (Sauber C20), 59 laps.

Schumacher led for the first four laps, but the decisive manner in which Häkkinen swooped past him to take the lead going into Becketts indicated that the Finn was not taking any prisoners and would not be denied. Mika dominated the race from there on, while Coulthard's hopes of rounding off a hat trick of McLaren victories ended after an early tangle with Jarno Trulli's Jordan.

2002, 7 July
SILVERSTONE, 60 laps of 3.194-mile circuit

1st, Michael Schumacher (Ferrari F2002), 1h 31m 45.015s, 125.3mph; 2nd, Rubens Barrichello (Ferrari F2002), 1h 31m 59.593s; 3rd, Juan Pablo Montoya (Williams FW24), 1h 32m 16.676s; 4th, Jacques Villeneuve (BAR 004), 59 laps; 5th, Olivier Panis (BAR 004), 59 laps; 6th, Nick Heidfeld (Sauber C21), 59 laps.

Montoya started from pole and kept his Williams-BMW ahead for 15 glorious laps, after which the Ferrari train took over at the front of the field. Villeneuve and Panis did a promising job to bring their BAR-Hondas home in the points, but McLaren had a bad day, with new recruit Kimi Räikkönen being sidelined by engine failure.

2003, 20 July
SILVERSTONE, 60 laps of 3.194-mile circuit

1st, Rubens Barrichello (Ferrari F2003-GA), 1h 28m 37.554s, 129.72mph; 2nd, Juan Pablo Montoya (Williams FW25), 1h 28m 43.016s; 3rd, Kimi Räikkönen (McLaren MP4-17D), 1h 28m 48.21s; 4th, Michael Schumacher (Ferrari F2003-GA), 1h 29m 3.202s; 5th, David Coulthard (McLaren MP4-17D), 1h 29m 14.381s; 6th, Jarno Trulli (Renault R23B), 1h 29m 20.621s.

A rare slip during qualifying put Michael Schumacher back in fifth place on the grid, which left pole-sitter Barrichello in a strong position. Once he got the upper hand in a mid-race tussle with Räikkönen, Rubens scored a well-paced win by just over 5 seconds from Montoya's Williams, the Colombian climbing through from seventh on the grid. Toyota driver Cristiano da Matta went well, briefly leading and finishing seventh.

2004, 11 July
SILVERSTONE, 60 laps of 3.194-mile circuit

1st, Michael Schumacher (Ferrari F2004), 1h 24m 42.7s, 135.71mph; 2nd, Kimi Räikkönen (McLaren MP4-19D), 1h 24m 44.830s; 3rd, Rubens Barrichello (Ferrari F2004), 1h 24m 45.814s; 4th, Jenson Button (BAR 006), 1h 24m 53.383s; 5th, Juan Pablo Montoya (Williams FW26), 1h 24m 54.873s; 6th, Giancarlo Fisichella (Sauber C23), 1h 24m 55.588s.

Räikkönen looked as though he might have the pace to beat Schumacher from pole position, but after he led for 11 laps Schumacher went ahead and stayed there until the chequered flag, although Kimi kept the pressure up all the way to the finish. Jenson Button was slightly disappointed not to manage better than fourth for BAR.

2005, 10 July
SILVERSTONE, 60 laps of 3.194-mile circuit

1st, Juan Pablo Montoya (McLaren MP4-20), 1h 24m 29.588s, 136.06mph; 2nd, Fernando Alonso (Renault R25), 1h 24m 32.327s; 3rd, Kimi Räikkönen (McLaren MP4-20), 1h 24m 44.024s; 4th, Giancarlo Fisichella (Renault R25), 1h 24m

47.502s; 5th, Jenson Button (BAR 007), 1h 25m 9.852s; 6th, Michael Schumacher (Ferrari F2005), 1h 25m 44.91s.

Alonso put his Renault commandingly on pole, but Montoya knew that the Spaniard was keeping his eye on his unfolding world championship prospects and correctly judged that he would not fight too hard as they muscled into the opening corner. The McLaren driver asserted himself with great confidence and style and his team-mate Räikkönen did well to finish third after taking an engine-change penalty that dropped him to 12th on the grid.

2006, 11 June
SILVERSTONE, 60 laps of 3.194-mile circuit
1st, Fernando Alonso (Renault R26), 1h 25m 51.927s, 133.89mph; 2nd, Michael Schumacher (Ferrari 248 F1), 1h 26m 5.878s; 3rd, Kimi Räikkönen (McLaren MP4-21), 1h 26m 10.599s; 4th, Giancarlo Fisichella (Renault R26), 1h 26m 11.903s; 5th, Felipe Massa (Ferrari 248 F1), 1h 26m 23.486s; 6th, Juan Pablo Montoya (McLaren MP4-21), 1h 26m 56.696s.

Had he so chosen, Fernando Alonso could have been back in his Oxford apartment in time for a late Sunday lunch after a brisk 90-minute workout to win the British Grand Prix for the first time in his career. Pre-race speculation that Schumacher and Räikkönen were running a fuel strategy that would allow them to out-fumble the world champion proved not to be the case.

2007, 8 July
SILVERSTONE, 59 laps of 3.194-mile circuit
1st, Kimi Räikkönen (Ferrari F2007), 1h 21m 43.074s,

138.335mph; 2nd, Fernando Alonso (McLaren MP4-22), 1h 21m 45.533s; 3rd, Lewis Hamilton (McLaren MP4-22), 1h 22m 22.447s; 4th, Robert Kubica (BMW Sauber F1.07), 1h 22m 36.393s; 5th, Felipe Massa (Ferrari F2007), 1h 22m 37.137s; 6th, Nick Heidfeld (BMW Sauber F1.07), 1h 22m 39.41s.

Lewis Hamilton's hopes of winning the British Grand Prix at his first attempt evaporated disappointingly into an eventual third place for McLaren, despite the fact that he started from pole position. Instead it was Räikkönen who became the first driver to win three races during the season so far as he vaulted his Ferrari ahead of Alonso's Renault at the final round of refuelling stops to finish ahead of the world champion.

2008, 6 July
SILVERSTONE, 60 laps of 3.194-mile circuit
1st, Lewis Hamilton (McLaren MP4-23), 1h 39m 9.44s, 115.94mph; 2nd, Nick Heidfeld (BMW Sauber F1.08), 1h 40m 18.017s; 3rd, Rubens Barrichello (Honda RA108), 1h 40m 31.713s; 4th, Kimi Räikkönen (Ferrari F2008), 59 laps; 5th, Heikki Kovalainen (McLaren MP4-23), 59 laps; 6th, Fernando Alonso (Renault R28), 59 laps.

After qualifying a lowly fourth, Lewis Hamilton rocketed straight through into the lead of this rain-soaked race, brushing aside his team-mate Heikki Kovalainen as the pack jostled into Copse corner. Heikki kept his nerve and stayed ahead, but Hamilton swooped by going into Stowe on lap five and that was the end of the story. Only Nick Heidfeld and Rubens Barrichello survived to finish on the same lap as Lewis.

2009, 21 July

SILVERSTONE, 70 laps of 3.194 circuit

1st Sebastian Vettel (Red Bull RB5), 1h 22m 49.328s, 138.81mph; 2nd, Mark Webber (Red Bull RB5), 1h 23m 4.516s; 3rd, Rubens Barrichello (Brawn BGP 001), 1h 23m 30.483s; 4th, Felipe Massa (Ferrari F60), 1h 23m 34.371s; 5th, Nico Rosberg (Williams FW310), 1h 23m 35.243s; 6th, Jenson Button (Brawn BGP 001), 1h 23m 35.613s.

A copy-book performance by the brilliant Vettel – he strengthened his reputation as one of the most exciting new talents to emerge on the F1 stage in recent years. Barrichello shone for Brawn to take third behind Webber, while Jenson Button could manage only sixth after qualifying was spoiled by handling problems.

APPENDIX 2

Dramatis personae

RAY BELLM

Accomplished sports car driver and three-times C2 world champion Ray Bellm was appointed chairman of the BRDC board in 2004 and variously described as an antidote to what some judged Jackie Stewart's overwhelming strength of personality or as a 'loose cannon', depending on your viewpoint. Energetic and enthusiastic, he clashed frequently with Stewart's more temperate approach during the crucial period in which the 2005–09 British Grand Prix contract was being negotiated and the longer-term future of Silverstone secured. He eventually attempted to unseat Stewart by urging members to demand his resignation on the basis that he should have left grand prix negotiations to the chief executive or the chairman.

At an extraordinary general meeting in May 2005 Sir Jackie won the members' support to stay on, effectively endorsing the earlier decision by the board to vote Bellm out of the post of chairman. After the endorsement of Sir Jackie by the membership, Bellm resigned from the BRDC board altogether.

ROBERT BROOKS

Former keen amateur racing driver who excelled in the auctioneering business and is now chairman of the prestigious

Bonhams auction house. Joined the BRDC board in 2005 and quickly proved himself to be an able negotiator and a popular personality with the members. Amused many of his board colleagues with his continuing and impassioned belief that associate members – of which I am one – should not have the vote when it comes to shaping club policy.

MARTIN BRUNDLE

Hugely respected as a versatile and accomplished racing driver, Brundle was one of the best F1 competitors of his generation never to win a world championship grand prix. The high point of his career came in the 1992 British Grand Prix at Silverstone when he drove his Benetton B192 to a storming third place behind the dominant Williams FW14Bs of Nigel Mansell and Riccardo Patrese, in the process beating his own team-mate Michael Schumacher into fourth place.

Brundle took over the role of BRDC chairman alongside new president Jackie Stewart in the early 1990s. He worked hard with Sir Jackie to promote and progress the so-called Silverstone master plan in the 1990s, which involved a proposed £80 million investment to upgrade the circuit to match anything that could then be found elsewhere in the world, but was frustrated by Bernie Ecclestone's reluctance to sign off and formally agree the master plan. He eventually stood down from the role of chairman because it was just taking too much of his business time, but is remembered by those who worked with him at the BRDC as a steadying influence and a perfect collaborator with Jackie Stewart during his time as president. He is now the voice of F1 on BBC television.

BERNIE ECCLESTONE

F1 commercial rights holder and the most powerful man on the international motor racing scene for the past 40 years. Before Bernie came on the scene, individual race organisers negotiated with individual teams on an ad hoc basis, creating a situation in which it was possible for prestigious teams such as Ferrari – in fact, usually Ferrari – to threaten organisers with their cars' non-attendance right up until the last minute because they concluded they would not be competitive at this particular race.

Ecclestone first established the predominantly Britain-based Formula One Constructors' Association as his power base during the 1970s, battling with FISA president Jean-Marie Balestre for control of F1's commercial rights. Ecclestone, a stake in whose business was acquired by CVC Capital Partners in 2005, now controls every commercial aspect of the F1 industry from television coverage contracts to corporate hospitality and trackside advertising. Often critical of the manner in which the BRDC managed its business at Silverstone, he pressured it relentlessly over the years to improve the circuit and its facilities.

NICOLA FOULSTON

High-achieving daughter of Atlantic Computers magnate John Foulston, who bought Brands Hatch in 1986 and was killed just over a year later when his McLaren Indycar crashed during testing at Silverstone. Nicola raised the finance to buy control of Brands Hatch and its associated businesses from her father's family trusts, which were by then controlled by her mother Mary. She successfully raised the prospect of returning the British Grand Prix to Brands Hatch after signing a deal with

Bernie Ecclestone and tried to buy Silverstone when it became clear that neither the necessary planning permission nor space to build the development would be available.

She sold the Brands Hatch Leisure group to the US Octagon Motorsports, a subsidiary of the giant New York-based Interpublic Group, and walked away from motor sport with enough cash to ensure that she would never have to work again, if she so chose.

SIMON GILLETT

Former Royal Navy weapons engineer who subsequently proved very successful in the retail business. His only previous contact with motor sport came through his father's position as head of sponsorship for the French Elf fuel and lubricants business in the UK. Backed by Monaco-based businessman Paul White, he failed in his efforts to move the British Grand Prix to Donington Park, claiming that Silverstone had a lucky break in that the effects of the economic recession caused the failure of Donington Ventures Leisure Ltd's plans and played right into Silverstone's hands.

ALEXANDER HESKETH

Best remembered for fielding James Hunt in the Hesketh Racing 308 back in the 1970s, running the team out of the stable block at Easton Neston, the Hesketh family home on the edge of Towcester, a mere two minutes' helicopter flight from the Silverstone paddock. Hesketh had a genuinely aristocratic demeanour that concealed a dry and ironic sense of humour and is remembered for his role as BRDC president as much with respect as with affection

DAMON HILL

Son of 1962 and 1968 world champion Graham Hill, who was killed in an air crash on Arkley golf course, north London, while returning from an F1 test session at Paul Ricard in 1975 when Damon was just 15. Having initially competed on motorcycles, Damon switched to four wheels and landed a job as Williams F1 test driver in 1992, before being promoted to the race team alongside Alain Prost the following year after Nigel Mansell opted to contest the 1993 US Indycar championship. He won the 1996 world championship for Williams and subsequently drove for Arrows and Jordan before retiring.

Calm, measured, and quite introspective, Damon was effectively Sir Jackie Stewart's nominated successor for the role of BRDC president when the Scot stood down in 2006. Imbued with an attractive line in ironic and self-deprecatory humour, Hill has proved both popular and successful in his role.

INNES IRELAND

Hugely popular and charismatic Scottish F1 driver who won the 1961 United States Grand Prix at Watkins Glen at the wheel of a Lotus 21, thereby achieving the Lotus factory team's maiden victory in a world championship-qualifying round. A prominent member of the BRDC with a great sporting ethic, Ireland was outraged by the events surrounding the so-called 'Walkinshaw affair', which led to some BRDC board members being sued by their own club in 1992–93 after the ill-starred sale of a 50 per cent stake in TWR's motor trading empire to the club. He took over as president after Jack Sears was ousted from the position, a position he held for less than a year before his death from cancer in late 1993.

JACK SEARS

An experienced and gregarious former semi-professional driver who raced for Team Lotus in sports and saloon cars during the 1960s. A Norfolk farmer by profession, he was president of the BRDC when the board plunged into the ill-starred Silverstone Motor Group business partnership with Tom Walkinshaw's TWR organisation in 1992. Sears was swept from office in the root-and-branch reorganisation that followed the membership's fury at the board's initial refusal to reveal how much it had paid for involvement in this fiasco. The club did eventually recoup its monies with costs after a prolonged legal action.

TOMMY SOPWITH

Son of aviation pioneer Sir Thomas Sopwith who invented the Sopwith Camel, the First World War fighter B-plane, Tommy Sopwith was an accomplished racing driver in his own right, a talented offshore powerboat racer, and an influential member of the BRDC board of directors in the early 1990s. He is also well acquainted personally with Bernie Ecclestone. In 1958 he went head-to-head with fellow BRDC member Jack Sears in a battle for the first British touring car championship, Sears racing an Austin A105 and Sopwith a 3.4-litre Jaguar in the bigger-engined class. Sears eventually took the championship in a tie decider at Brands Hatch after the two men competed in a two-car event with rally specification Riley 1.5-litre saloons.

Sopwith has a Brighton car dealership. His father left a large Hampshire estate (sold a year later for £12 million), a Scottish castle, and more property in Yorkshire and the Bahamas when he died in 1989, aged 101. Endeavour Holdings, Sopwith's company, made a £724,000 profit on sales of £10.4 million in

2007. It was then said to be worth £15 million and controlled other interests, such as the Longshot restaurant operation.

Before Nicola Foulston made an offer for the British Grand Prix, Sopwith went with Denys Rohan as a BRDC emissary to Ecclestone's London office at Princes Gate to discuss what figure he might realistically settle on to keep the British Grand Prix. Ecclestone recalls that he offered Sopwith the chance of doing a deal for the same price as the cheapest current European race. But Sopwith decided it was still too costly for the club.

SIR JACKIE STEWART

Triple F1 world champion who retired from racing at the end of 1973 and has since become one of the sport's most recognisable business personalities and opinion formers. His distinguished career behind the wheel yielded a then-record 27 grand prix victories and he campaigned tirelessly for dramatically enhanced motor racing safety, both in terms of circuits and in constructional aspects of the cars.

Stewart succeeded Ken Tyrrell as president of the BRDC in 2000, holding the position for six years, during which period he deployed the same relentless drive and attention to detail that characterised his career at the wheel. He is very hot on correct corporate governance and the need for any business he is involved in not only to do the correct things but to do them in the right way, and was one of the driving forces behind renewing the British Grand Prix contract at Silverstone from 2005 to 2009.

Both being highly competitive and driven men, it was no surprise that Stewart and Bernie Ecclestone had a sometimes tense and even tetchy relationship, although it was buttressed by an underlying mood of mutual respect for what the other had achieved. They both drove a hard bargain and were highly competitive operators throughout the battle for the British Grand Prix.

KEN TYRRELL

Highly respected F1 team owner who followed Alexander Hesketh as president of the BRDC in the late 1990s. Suffering from cancer, he persuaded Jackie Stewart to follow him into that position when he stood down in 2000, just over a year before he died. A bluff, outspoken, and very honest man, he did his best to steer the BRDC away from the rocks during one of the most difficult periods in its history.

TOM WALKINSHAW

Tough and uncompromising, both as a businessman and as a racing driver, Walkinshaw and his TWR empire will be recalled by many as the driving power that put Jaguar back on the international sports car racing scene in the 1980s. He was later involved with the Benetton and Arrows F1 teams. His relationship with the BRDC on the business front was considerably more controversial, involving as it did the sale of a 50 per cent stake in his car retailing business, for which the club paid in excess of £5 million after being incorrectly advised by its solicitors that prior approval of the deal would not have to be secured from the voting membership.

JOHN WEBB

Started life in motor sport as press officer at Brands Hatch during the 1950s and rose to be managing director of track owners Motor Circuit Developments. An astute businessman with an intuitive feel for what would entertain the paying public, for more than two decades Webb was one of the genuinely promotional visionaries within the sport, conjuring up a wide range of ideas, from the traditional Boxing Day Brands Hatch meeting to the Rothmans 50,000 super formule libre race, which attracted a huge field in 1972. He attempted to broker a 50–50 acquisition of Brands Hatch by Ecclestone with John Foulston and was dismayed when it fell through. He retired with his wife Angela to Spain.

TOM WHEATCROFT
Rough, tough, and charismatic Leicester building contractor who was inspired as a schoolboy by the sight of the German Auto Unions and Mercedes competing in the pre-war Donington Grands Prix and who later spent some of his fortune purchasing the run-down circuit near Derby, finally reviving it for racing in 1977. He realised a personal dream when he was able to stage the European Grand Prix at his revamped circuit in 1993, won brilliantly in the pouring rain by Ayrton Senna's McLaren. Tom eventually sold a long-term lease on the circuit to Simon Gillett's Donington Ventures Leisure organisation, which signed a long-term contract to stage the British Grand Prix from 2010 but spectacularly failed to deliver on that commitment.

BIBLIOGRAPHY

The following titles are mentioned in this book:

John Blunsden, *Silverstone: Fifty Glorious Years*, Motor Racing Publications, 1998

Maurice Hamilton, *British Grand Prix*, Crowood Press, 1989

Terry Lovell, *Bernie Ecclestone: King of Sport*, John Blake, 2008

Sir Stirling Moss, *All My Races*, Haynes, 2009

Sir Jackie Stewart, *Winning is Not Enough: The Autobiography* (© Sir Jackie Stewart, 2007), first published in the UK by Headline Publishing Group Ltd, 338 Euston Road, London NW1 3BH

INDEX

234